Benita
An African Romance

by

H. Rider Haggard

Double 9
BOOKS

Benita
An African Romance
by H. Rider Haggard

Copyright © 2024

ISBN: 978-93-57485-70-8

Published by

DOUBLE 9 BOOKS

2/13-B, Ansari Road
Daryaganj, New Delhi – 110002
info@double9books.com
www.double9books.com
Tel. 011-40042856

ABOUT THE AUTHOR

H. Rider Haggard was born on 22 June, 1856 in Braden ham, situated in the English area of Norfolk. His father, Sir William Meybohm Rider Haggard, was a lawyer, while his mother, Ella Dove ton Haggard, was an author herself. The couple had ten children, out of which Henry was conceived as the eighth. Sir Henry Rider Haggard was an English author who was known for his African thriller novel, 'Lord Solomon's Mines'. His father was a Norfolk advocate but he was denied an honourable men's schooling compared to his siblings due to his physical bluntness. At 19 years old, he started his vocation at the command of his father as an unpaid guide to Lieutenant-Governor of the Colony of Natal. Rider Haggard was married to a Norfolk beneficiary Marianna Louisa Margitson. They had four children named Jack, who died at the age of 10 due to measles, and three girls named Angela, Dorothy, and Lilias. Rider Haggard died at the age of 68 in London. His remains were cremated at St Mary's Church, Ditchingham. A rail route point of the Canadian National Railway in British Columbia has been named after him.

CONTENTS

I.   CONFIDENCES 7

II.   THE END OF THE "ZANZIBAR." 17

III.   HOW ROBERT CAME ASHORE 25

IV.   MR. CLIFFORD 33

V.   JACOB MEYER 42

VI.   THE GOLD COIN 51

VII.   THE MESSENGERS 59

VIII.   BAMBATSE 67

IX.   THE OATH OF MADUNA 76

X.   THE MOUNTAIN TOP 84

XI.   THE SLEEPERS IN THE CAVE 92

XII.   THE BEGINNING OF THE SEARCH 100

XIII.   BENITA PLANS ESCAPE 108

XIV.   THE FLIGHT 116

XV.   THE CHASE 124

XVI.   BACK AT BAMBATSE 132

XVII.	THE FIRST EXPERIMENT	140
XVIII.	THE OTHER BENITA	147
XIX.	THE AWAKING	157
XX.	JACOB MEYER SEES A SPIRIT	165
XXI.	THE MESSAGE FROM THE DEAD	173
XXII.	THE VOICE OF THE LIVING	181
XXIII.	BENITA GIVES HER ANSWER	189
XXIV.	THE TRUE GOLD	197

I.
CONFIDENCES

Beautiful, beautiful was that night! No air that stirred; the black smoke from the funnels of the mail steamer *Zanzibar* lay low over the surface of the sea like vast, floating ostrich plumes that vanished one by one in the starlight. Benita Beatrix Clifford, for that was her full name, who had been christened Benita after her mother and Beatrix after her father's only sister, leaning idly over the bulwark rail, thought to herself that a child might have sailed that sea in a boat of bark and come safely into port.

Then a tall man of about thirty years of age, who was smoking a cigar, strolled up to her. At his coming she moved a little as though to make room for him beside her, and there was something in the motion which, had anyone been there to observe it, might have suggested that these two were upon terms of friendship, or still greater intimacy. For a moment he hesitated, and while he did so an expression of doubt, of distress even, gathered on his face. It was as though he understood that a great deal depended on whether he accepted or declined that gentle invitation, and knew not which to do.

Indeed, much did depend upon it, no less than the destinies of both of them. If Robert Seymour had gone by to finish his cigar in solitude, why then this story would have had a very different ending; or, rather, who can say how it might have ended? The dread, foredoomed event with which that night was big would have come to its awful birth leaving certain words unspoken. Violent separation must have ensued, and even if both of them had survived the terror, what prospect was there that their lives would again have crossed each other in that wide Africa?

But it was not so fated, for just as he put his foot forward to continue his march Benita spoke in her low and pleasant voice.

"Are you going to the smoking-room or to the saloon to dance, Mr. Seymour? One of the officers just told me that there is to be a dance," she added, in explanation, "because it is so calm that we might fancy ourselves ashore."

"Neither," he answered. "The smoking-room is stuffy, and my dancing days are over. No; I proposed to take exercise after that big dinner, and then to sit in a chair and fall asleep. But," he added, and his voice grew interested, "how did you know that it was I? You never turned your head."

"I have ears in my head as well as eyes," she answered with a little laugh, "and after we have been nearly a month together on this ship I ought to know your step."

"I never remember that anyone ever recognized it before," he said, more to himself than to her, then came and leaned over the rail at her side. His doubts were gone. Fate had spoken.

For a while there was silence between them, then he asked her if she were not going to the dance.

Benita shook her head.

"Why not? You are fond of dancing, and you dance very well. Also there are plenty of officers for partners, especially Captain— —" and he checked himself.

"I know," she said; "it would be pleasant, but—Mr. Seymour, will you think me foolish if I tell you something?"

"I have never thought you foolish yet, Miss Clifford, so I don't know why I should begin now. What is it?"

"I am not going to the dance because I am afraid, yes, horribly afraid."

"Afraid! Afraid of what?"

"I don't quite know, but, Mr. Seymour, I feel as though we were all of us upon the edge of some dreadful catastrophe—as though there were about to be a mighty change, and beyond it another life, something new and unfamiliar. It came over me at dinner—that was why I left the table. Quite suddenly I looked, and all the people were different, yes, all except a few."

"Was I different?" he asked curiously.

"No, you were not," and he thought he heard her add "Thank God!" beneath her breath.

"And were you different?"

"I don't know. I never looked at myself; I was the seer, not the seen. I have always been like that."

"Indigestion," he said reflectively. "We eat too much on board ship, and the dinner was very long and heavy. I told you so, that's why I'm taking—I mean why I wanted to take exercise."

"And to go to sleep afterwards."

"Yes, first the exercise, then the sleep. Miss Clifford, that is the rule of life—and death. With sleep thought ends, therefore for some of us your catastrophe is much to be desired, for it would mean long sleep and no thought."

"I said that they were changed, not that they had ceased to think. Perhaps they thought the more."

"Then let us pray that your catastrophe may be averted. I prescribe for you bismuth and carbonate of soda. Also in this weather it seems difficult to imagine such a thing. Look now, Miss Clifford," he added, with a note of enthusiasm in his voice, pointing towards the east, "look."

Her eyes followed his outstretched hand, and there, above the level ocean, rose the great orb of the African moon. Lo! of a sudden all that ocean turned to silver, a wide path of rippling silver stretched from it to them. It might have been the road of angels. The sweet soft light beat upon their ship, showing its tapering masts and every detail of the rigging. It passed on beyond them, and revealed the low, foam-fringed coast-line rising here and there, dotted with kloofs and their clinging bush. Even the round huts of Kaffir kraals became faintly visible in that radiance. Other things became visible also—for instance, the features of this pair.

The man was light in his colouring, fair-skinned, with fair hair which already showed a tendency towards greyness, especially in the moustache, for he wore no beard. His face was clean cut, not particularly handsome, since, their fineness notwithstanding, his features lacked regularity; the cheekbones were too high and the chin was too small, small faults redeemed to some extent by the steady and cheerful grey eyes. For the rest, he was broad-shouldered and well-set-up, sealed with the indescribable stamp of the English gentleman. Such was the appearance of Robert Seymour.

In that light the girl at his side looked lovely, though, in fact, she had no real claims to loveliness, except perhaps as regards her figure, which was agile, rounded, and peculiarly graceful. Her foreign-looking face was unusual, dark-eyed, a somewhat large and very mobile mouth, fair and waving hair, a broad forehead, a sweet and at times wistful face, thoughtful for the most part, but apt to be irradiated by sudden smiles. Not a beautiful woman at all, but exceedingly attractive, one possessing magnetism.

She gazed, first at the moon and the silver road beneath it, then, turning, at the land beyond.

"We are very near to Africa, at last," she said.

"Too near, I think," he answered. "If I were the captain I should stand out a point or two. It is a strange country, full of surprises. Miss Clifford, will you think me rude if I ask you why you are going there? You have never told me—quite."

"No, because the story is rather a sad one; but you shall hear it if you wish. Do you?"

He nodded, and drew up two deck chairs, in which they settled themselves in a corner made by one of the inboard boats, their faces still towards the sea.

"You know I was born in Africa," she said, "and lived there till I was thirteen years old—why, I find I can still speak Zulu; I did so this afternoon. My father was one of the early settlers in Natal. His father was a clergyman, a younger son of the Lincolnshire Cliffords. They are great people there still, though I don't suppose that they are aware of my existence."

"I know them," answered Robert Seymour. "Indeed, I was shooting at their place last November—when the smash came," and he sighed; "but go on."

"Well, my father quarrelled with his father, I don't know what about, and emigrated. In Natal he married my mother, a Miss Ferreira, whose name—like mine and her mother's—was Benita. She was one of two sisters, and her father, Andreas Ferreira, who married an English lady, was half Dutch and half Portuguese. I remember him well, a fine old man with dark eyes and an iron-grey beard. He was wealthy as things went in those days—that is to say, he had lots of land in Natal and the Transvaal, and great herds of stock. So you see I am half English, some Dutch, and more than a quarter Portuguese—quite a mixture of races. My father and mother did not get on well together. Mr. Seymour, I may as well tell you all the truth: he drank, and although he was passionately fond of her, she was jealous of him. Also he gambled away most of her patrimony, and after old Andreas Ferreira's death they grew poor. One night there was a dreadful scene between them, and in his madness he struck her.

"Well, she was a very proud woman, determined, too, and she turned on him and said—for I heard her—'I will never forgive you; we have done with each other.' Next morning, when my father was sober, he begged her pardon, but she made no answer, although he was starting somewhere on a fortnight's trek. When he had gone my mother ordered the Cape cart, packed up her clothes, took some money that she had put away, drove to Durban, and after making arrangements at the bank about a small private income of her own, sailed with me for England, leaving a letter for my father in which she said that she would never see him again, and if he tried to interfere with me she would put me under the protection of the English court, which would not allow me to be taken to the home of a drunkard.

"In England we went to live in London with my aunt, who had married a Major King, but was a widow with five children. My father often wrote to persuade my mother to go back to him, but she never would, which I think was wrong of her. So things went on for twelve years or more, till one day my mother suddenly died, and I came into her little fortune of between £200 and £300 a year, which she had tied up so that nobody can touch it. That was about a year ago. I wrote to tell my father of her death, and received a pitiful letter; indeed, I have had several of them. He implored me to come out to him and not to leave him to die in his loneliness, as he soon would do of a broken heart, if I did not. He said that he had long ago given up drinking, which was the cause of the ruin of his life, and sent a certificate signed by a magistrate and a doctor to that effect. Well, in the end, although all my cousins and their mother advised me against it, I consented, and here I am. He is to meet me at Durban, but how we shall get on together is more than I can say, though I long to see him, for after all he is my father."

"It was good of you to come, under all the circumstances. You must have a brave heart," said Robert reflectively.

"It is my duty," she answered. "And for the rest, I am not afraid who was born to Africa. Indeed, often and often have I wished to be back there again, out on the veld, far away from the London streets and fog. I am young and strong, and I want to see things, natural things—not those made by man, you know—the things I remember as a child. One can always go back to London."

"Yes, or at least some people can. It is a curious thing, Miss Clifford, but as it happens I have met your father. You always reminded me of the man, but I had forgotten his name. Now it comes back to me; it *was* Clifford."

"Where on earth?" she asked, astonished.

"In a queer place. As I told you, I have visited South Africa before, under different circumstances. Four years ago I was out here big-game shooting. Going in from the East coast my brother and I—he is dead now, poor fellow—got up somewhere in the Matabele country, on the banks of the Zambesi. As we didn't find much game there we were going to strike south, when some natives told us of a wonderful ruin that stood on a hill overhanging the river a few miles farther on. So, leaving the waggon on the hither side of the steep nek, over which it would have been difficult to drag it, my brother and I took our rifles and a bag of food and started. The place was farther off than we thought, although from the top of the nek we could see it clearly enough, and before we reached it dark had fallen.

"Now we had observed a waggon and a tent outside the wall which we thought must belong to white men, and headed for them. There was a light in the tent, and the flap was open, the night being very hot. Inside two men were seated, one old, with a grey beard, and the other, a good-looking fellow—under forty, I should say—with a Jewish face, dark, piercing eyes, and a black, pointed beard. They were engaged in examining a heap of gold beads and bangles, which lay on the table between them. As I was about to speak, the black-bearded man heard or caught sight of us, and seizing a rifle that leaned against the table, swung round and covered me.

"'For God's sake don't shoot, Jacob,' said the old man; 'they are English.'

"'Best dead, any way,' answered the other, in a soft voice, with a slight foreign accent, 'we don't want spies or thieves here.'

"'We are neither, but I can shoot as well as you, friend,' I remarked, for by this time my rifle was on him.

"Then he thought better of it, and dropped his gun, and we explained that we were merely on an archæological expedition. The end of it was that we became capital friends, though neither of us could cotton much to Mr. Jacob—I forget his other name. He struck me as too handy with his rifle, and was, I gathered, an individual with a mysterious and rather lurid past. To cut a long story short, when he found out that we had no intention of poaching, your father, for it was he, told us frankly that they were treasure-hunting, having got hold of some story about a vast store of gold which had been hidden away there by Portuguese two or three centuries before. Their trouble was, however, that the Makalanga, who lived in the fortress, which was called Bambatse, would not allow them to dig, because they said the place was haunted, and if they did so it would bring bad luck to their tribe."

"And did they ever get in?" asked Benita.

"I am sure I don't know, for we went next day, though before we left we called on the Makalanga, who admitted us all readily enough so long as we brought no spades with us. By the way, the gold we saw your father and his friend examining was found in some ancient graves outside the walls, but had nothing to do with the big and mythical treasure."

"What was the place like? I love old ruins," broke in Benita again.

"Oh! wonderful. A gigantic, circular wall built by heaven knows who, then half-way up the hill another wall, and near the top a third wall which, I understood, surrounded a sort of holy of holies, and above everything, on the brink of the precipice, a great cone of granite."

"Artificial or natural?"

"I don't know. They would not let us up there, but we were introduced to their chief and high priest, Church and State in one, and a wonderful old man he was, very wise and very gentle. I remember he told me he believed we should meet again, which seemed an odd thing for him to say. I asked him about the treasure and why he would not let the other white men look for it. He answered that it would never be found by any man, white or black, that only a woman would find it at the appointed time, when it pleased the Spirit of Bambatse, under whose guardianship it was."

"Who was the Spirit of Bambatse, Mr. Seymour?"

"I can't tell you, couldn't make out anything definite about her, except that she was said to be white, and to appear sometimes at sunrise, or in the moonlight, standing upon the tall point of rock of which I told you. I remember that I got up before the dawn to look for her—like an idiot, for of course I saw nothing—and that's all I know about the matter."

"Did you have any talk with my father, Mr. Seymour—alone, I mean?"

"Yes, a little. The next day he walked back to our waggon with us, being glad, I fancy, of a change from the perpetual society of his partner Jacob. That wasn't wonderful in a man who had been brought up at Eton and Oxford, as I found out he had, like myself, and whatever his failings may have been—although we saw no sign of them, for he would not touch a drop of spirits—was a gentleman, which Jacob wasn't. Still, he—Jacob—had read a lot, especially on out-of-the-way subjects, and could talk every language under the sun—a clever and agreeable scoundrel in short."

"Did my father say anything about himself?"

"Yes; he told me that he had been an unsuccessful man all his life, and had much to reproach himself with, for we got quite confidential at last. He added that he had a family in England—what family he didn't say—whom he was anxious to make wealthy by way of reparation for past misdeeds, and that was why he was treasure-hunting. However, from what you tell me, I fear he never found anything."

"No, Mr. Seymour, he never found it and never will, but all the same I am glad to hear that he was thinking of us. Also I should like to explore that place, Bambatse."

"So should I, Miss Clifford, in your company, and your father's, but not in that of Jacob. If ever you should go there with him, I say:— 'Beware of Jacob.'"

"Oh! I am not afraid of Jacob," she answered with a laugh, "although I believe that my father still has something to do with him—at least in one of his letters he mentioned his partner, who was a German."

"A German! I think that he must have meant a German Jew."

After this there was silence between them for a time, then he said suddenly, "You have told me your story, would you like to hear mine?"

"Yes," she answered.

"Well, it won't take you long to listen to it, for, Miss Clifford, like Canning's needy knife-grinder, I have really none to tell. You see before you one of the most useless persons in the world, an undistinguished member of what is called in England the 'leisured class,' who can do absolutely nothing that is worth doing, except shoot straight."

"Indeed," said Benita.

"You do not seem impressed with that accomplishment," he went on, "yet it is an honest fact that for the last fifteen years—I was thirty-two this month—practically my whole time has been given up to it, with a little fishing thrown in in the spring. As I want to make the most of myself, I will add that I am supposed to be among the six best shots in England, and that my ambition—yes, great Heavens! my ambition—was to become better than the other five. By that sin fell the poor man who speaks to you. I was supposed to have abilities, but I neglected them all to pursue this form of idleness. I entered no profession, I did no work, with the result that at thirty-two I am ruined and almost hopeless."

"Why ruined and hopeless?" she asked anxiously, for the way in which they were spoken grieved her more than the words themselves.

"Ruined because my old uncle, the Honourable John Seymour Seymour, whose heir I was, committed the indiscretion of marrying a young lady who has presented him with thriving twins. With the appearance of those twins my prospects disappeared, as did the allowance of £1,500 a year that he was good enough to make me on which to keep up a position as his next-of-kin. I had something of my own, but also I had debts, and at the present moment a draft in my pocket for £2,163 14s. 5d., and a little loose cash, represents the total of my worldly goods, just about the sum I have been accustomed to spend per annum."

"I don't call that ruin, I call that riches," said Benita, relieved. "With £2,000 to begin on you may make a fortune in Africa. But how about the hopelessness?"

"I am hopeless because I have absolutely nothing to which to look forward. Really, when that £2,000 is gone I do not know how to earn a sixpence. In this dilemma it occurred to me that the only thing I could do was to turn my shooting to practical account, and become a hunter of big game. Therefore I propose to kill elephants until an elephant kills me. At least," he added in a changed voice, "I did so propose until half an hour ago."

II.
THE END OF THE "ZANZIBAR."

"Until half an hour ago? Then why——" and Benita stopped.

"Have I changed my very modest scheme of life? Miss Clifford, as you are so good as to be sufficiently interested, I will tell you. It is because a temptation which hitherto I have been able to resist, has during the last thirty minutes become too strong for me. You know everything has its breaking strain." He puffed nervously at his cigar, threw it into the sea, paused, then went on: "Miss Clifford, I have dared to fall in love with you. No; hear me out. When I have done it will be quite time enough to give me the answer that I expect. Meanwhile, for the first time in my life, allow me the luxury of being in earnest. To me it is a new sensation, and therefore very priceless. May I go on?"

Benita made no answer. He rose with a certain deliberateness which characterized all his movements—for Robert Seymour never seemed to be in a hurry—and stood in front of her so that the moonlight shone upon her face, while his own remained in shadow.

"Beyond that £2,000 of which I have spoken, and incidentally its owner, I have nothing whatsoever to offer to you. I am an indigent and worthless person. Even in my prosperous days, when I could look forward to a large estate, although it was often suggested to me, I never considered myself justified in asking any lady to share—the prospective estate. I think now that the real reason was that I never cared sufficiently for any lady, since otherwise my selfishness would probably have overcome my scruples, as it does to-night. Benita, for I will call you so, if for the first and last time, I—I—love you.

"Listen now," he went on, dropping his measured manner, and speaking hurriedly, like a man with an earnest message and little time in which to deliver it, "it is an odd thing, an incomprehensible thing, but true, true—I fell in love with you the first time I saw your face.

You remember, you stood there leaning over the bulwark when I came on board at Southampton, and as I walked up the gangway, I looked and my eyes met yours. Then I stopped, and that stout old lady who got off at Madeira bumped into me, and asked me to be good enough to make up my mind if I were going backward or forward. Do you remember?"

"Yes," she answered in a low voice.

"Which things are an allegory," he continued. "I felt it so at the time. Yes, I had half a mind to answer 'Backward' and give up my berth in this ship. Then I looked at you again, and something inside of me said 'Forward.' So I came up the rest of the gangway and took off my hat to you, a salutation I had no right to make, but which, I recall, you acknowledged."

He paused, then continued: "As it began, so it has gone on. It is always like that, is it not? The beginning is everything, the end must follow. And now it has come out, as I was fully determined that it should not do half an hour ago, when suddenly you developed eyes in the back of your head, and—oh! dearest, I love you. No, please be quiet; I have not done. I have told you what I am, and really there isn't much more to say about me, for I have no particular vices except the worst of them all, idleness, and not the slightest trace of any virtue that I can discover. But I have a certain knowledge of the world acquired in a long course of shooting parties, and as a man of the world I will venture to give you a bit of advice. It is possible that to you my life and death affair is a mere matter of board-ship amusement. Yet it is possible also that you might take another view of the matter. In that case, as a friend and a man of the world, I entreat you—don't. Have nothing to do with me. Send me about my business; you will never regret it."

"Are you making fun, or is all this meant, Mr. Seymour?" asked Benita, still speaking beneath her breath, and looking straight before her.

"Meant? Of course it is meant. How can you ask?"

"Because I have always understood that on such occasions people wish to make the best of themselves."

"Quite so, but I never do what I ought, a fact for which I am grateful now come to think of it, since otherwise I should not be here to-night.

I wish to make the worst of myself, the very worst, for whatever I am not, at least I am honest. Now having told you that I am, or was half an hour ago, an idler, a good-for-nothing, prospectless failure, I ask you—if you care to hear any more?"

She half rose, and, glancing at him for the first time, saw his face contract itself and turn pale in the moonlight. It may be that the sight of it affected her, even to the extent of removing some adverse impression left by the bitter mocking of his self-blame. At any rate, Benita seemed to change her mind, and sat down again, saying:

"Go on, if you wish."

He bowed slightly, and said:

"I thank you. I have told you what I *was* half an hour ago; now, hoping that you will believe me, I will tell you what I *am*. I am a truly repentant man, one upon whom a new light has risen. I am not very old, and I think that underneath it all I have some ability. Opportunity may still come my way; if it does not, for your sake I will make the opportunity. I do not believe that you can ever find anyone who would love you better or care for you more tenderly. I desire to live for you in the future, more completely even than in the past I have lived for myself. I do not wish to influence you by personal appeals, but in fact I stand at the parting of the ways. If you will give yourself to me I feel as though I might still become a husband of whom you could be proud—if not, I write 'Finis' upon the tombstone of the possibilities of Robert Seymour. I adore you. You are the one woman with whom I desire to pass my days; it is you who have always been lacking to my life. I ask you to be brave, to take the risk of marrying me, although I can see nothing but poverty ahead of us, for I am an adventurer."

"Don't speak like that," she said quickly. "We are all of us adventurers in this world, and I more than you. We have just to consider ourselves, not what we have or have not."

"So be it, Miss Clifford. Then I have nothing more to say; now it is for you to answer."

Just then the sound of the piano and the fiddle in the saloon ceased. One of the waltzes was over, and some of the dancers came upon deck to flirt or to cool themselves. One pair, engaged very obviously in the former occupation, stationed themselves so near to Robert and Benita that further conversation between them was impossible, and there proceeded to interchange the remarks common to such occasions.

For a good ten minutes did they stand thus, carrying on a mock quarrel as to a dance of which one of them was supposed to have been defrauded, until Robert Seymour, generally a very philosophical person, could have slain those innocent lovers. He felt, he knew not why, that his chances were slipping away from him; that sensation of something bad about to happen, of which Benita had spoken, spread from her to him. The suspense grew exasperating, terrible even, nor could it be ended. To ask her to come elsewhere was under the circumstances not feasible, especially as he would also have been obliged to request the other pair to make way for them, and all this time, with a sinking of the heart, he felt that probably Benita was beating down any tenderness which she might feel towards him; that when her long-delayed answer did come the chances were it would be "No."

The piano began to play again in the saloon, and the young people, still squabbling archly, at length prepared to depart. Suddenly there was a stir upon the bridge, and against the tender sky Robert saw a man dash forward. Next instant the engine-room bell rang fiercely. He knew the signal—it was "Stop," followed at once by other ringings that meant "Full speed astern."

"I wonder what is up?" said the young man to the young woman.

Before the words had left his lips they knew. There was a sensation as though all the hull of the great ship had come to a complete standstill, while the top part of her continued to travel forward; followed by another sensation still more terrible and sickening in its nature—that of slipping over something, helplessly, heavily, as a man slips upon ice or a polished floor. Spars cracked, ropes flew in two with a noise as of pistol shots. Heavy objects rushed about the deck, travelling forwards all of them. Benita was hurled from her chair against Robert so that the two of them rolled into the scuppers. He was unhurt and picked himself up, but she lay still, and he saw that something had struck her upon the head, for blood was running down her cheek. He lifted her, and, filled with black horror and despair—for he thought her gone—pressed his hand upon her heart. Thank God! it began to beat again—she still lived.

The music in the saloon had stopped, and for a little while there was silence. Then of an instant there arose the horrible clamour of shipwreck; wild-eyed people rushed to and fro aimlessly; here and there women and children shrieked; a clergyman fell upon his knees and began to pray.

This went on for a space, till presently the second officer appeared and, affecting an unconcerned air, called out that it was all right, the captain said no one was to be afraid. He added that they were not more than six miles from the shore, and that the ship would be beached in half an hour. Indeed, as he spoke the engines, which had been stopped, commenced to work again, and her head swung round in a wide circle, pointing to the land. Evidently they had passed over the rock and were once more in deep water, through which they travelled at a good speed but with a heavy list to starboard. The pumps got to work also with a monotonous, clanging beat, throwing out great columns of foaming water on to the oily sea. Men began to cut the covers off the boats, and to swing some of them outboard. Such were the things that went on about them.

With the senseless Benita clasped to his breast, the blood from her cut head running down his shoulder, Robert stood still awhile, thinking. Then he made up his mind. As it chanced, she had a deck cabin, and thither he forced his way, carrying her tenderly and with patience through the distracted throng of passengers, for there were five hundred souls on board that ship. He reached the place to find that it was quite empty, her cabinmate having fled. Laying Benita upon the lower bunk, he lit the swinging candle. As soon as it burned up he searched for the lifebelts and by good fortune found two of them, one of which, not without great difficulty, he succeeded in fastening round her. Then he took a sponge and bathed her head with water. There was a great bruise upon her temple where the block or whatever it was had struck her, and the blood still flowed; but the wound was not very deep or extensive, nor, so far as he could discover, did the bone appear to be broken or driven in. He had good hope that she was only stunned, and would revive presently. Unable to do more for her, a thought struck him. On the floor of the cabin, thrown by the shock from the rack, lay her writing case. He opened it, and taking a piece of paper wrote these words hurriedly in pencil:

"You gave me no answer, and it is more than probable that I shall receive none in this world which one or both of us may be upon the verge of leaving. In the latter case we can settle the matter elsewhere — perhaps. In the former, should it be my lot to go and yours to stay, I hope that you will think kindly of me at times as of one who loved you truly. Should it be yours to go, then you will never read these words. Yet if to the dead is given knowledge, be assured that as you left me so you shall find me, yours and yours alone. Or perhaps we both may live; I pray so. —S. R. S."

Folding up the paper, he undid a button of Benita's blouse and thrust it away there, knowing that thus she would certainly find it should she survive. Then he stepped out on to the deck to see what was happening. The vessel still steamed, but made slow progress; moreover, the list to starboard was now so pronounced that it was difficult to stand upright. On account of it nearly all the passengers were huddled together upon the port side, having instinctively taken refuge as far as possible above the water. A man with a white, distraught face staggered towards him, supporting himself by the bulwarks. It was the captain. For a moment he paused as though to think, holding to a stanchion. Robert Seymour saw his opportunity and addressed him.

"Forgive me," he said; "I do not like interfering with other people's business, but for reasons unconnected with myself I suggest to you that it would be wise to stop this ship and get out the boats. The sea is calm; if it is not left till too late there should be no difficulty in launching them."

The man stared at him absently, then said:

"They won't hold everybody, Mr. Seymour. I hope to beach her."

"At least they will hold some," he answered, "whereas — —" And he pointed to the water, which by now was almost level with the deck.

"Perhaps you are right, Mr. Seymour. It doesn't matter to me, anyway. I am a ruined man; but the poor passengers — the poor passengers!" And he scrambled away fiercely towards the bridge like a wounded cat along the bough of a tree, whence in a few seconds Robert heard him shouting orders.

A minute or so afterwards the steamer stopped. Too late the captain had decided to sacrifice his ship and save those she carried.

They were beginning to get out the boats. Now Robert returned to the cabin where Benita was lying senseless, and wrapped her up in a cloak and some blankets. Then, seeing the second lifebelt on the floor, by an afterthought he put it on, knowing that there was time to spare. Next he lifted Benita, and feeling sure that the rush would be for the starboard side, on which the boats were quite near the water, carried her, with difficulty, for the slope was steep, to the port-cutter, which he knew would be in the charge of a good man, the second officer, whom he had seen in command there at Sunday boat-drills.

Here, as he had anticipated, the crowd was small, since most people thought that it would not be possible to get this boat down safely to the water; or if their powers of reflection were gone, instinct told them so. That skilful seaman, the second officer, and his appointed crew, were already at work lowering the cutter from the davits.

"Now," he said, "women and children first."

A number rushed in, and Robert saw that the boat would soon be full.

"I am afraid," he said, "that I must count myself a woman as I carry one," and by a great effort, holding Benita with one arm, with the other he let himself down the falls and, assisted by a quartermaster, gained the boat in safety.

One or two other men scrambled after him.

"Push her off," said the officer; "she can hold no more," and the ropes were let go.

When they were about twelve feet from the ship's side, from which they thrust themselves clear with oars, there came a rush of people, disappointed of places in the starboard boats. A few of the boldest of these swarmed down the falls, others jumped and fell among them, or missed and dropped into the sea, or struck upon the sides of the boat and were killed. Still she reached the water upon an even keel, though now much overladen. The oars were got out, and they rowed round the bow of the great ship wallowing in her death-throes, their first idea being to make for the shore, which was not three miles away.

This brought them to the starboard side, where they saw a hideous scene. Hundreds of people seemed to be fighting for room, with the result that some of the boats were overturned, precipitating their occupants into the water. Others hung by the prow or the stern, the ropes having jammed in the davits in the frantic haste and confusion, while from them human beings dropped one by one. Round others not yet launched a hellish struggle was in progress, the struggle of men, women, and children battling for their lives, in which the strong, mad with terror, showed no mercy to the weak.

From that mass of humanity, most of them about to perish, went up a babel of sounds which in its sum shaped itself to one prolonged scream, such as might proceed from a Titan in his agony. All this beneath a brooding, moonlit sky, and on a sea as smooth as glass. Upon the ship, which now lay upon her side, the siren still sent up its yells for succour, and some brave man continued to fire rockets, which rushed heavenwards and burst in showers of stars.

Robert remembered that the last rocket he had seen was fired at an evening *fête* for the amusement of the audience. The contrast struck him as dreadful. He wondered whether there were any power or infernal population that could be amused by a tragedy such as enacted itself before his eyes; how it came about also that such a tragedy was permitted by the merciful Strength in which mankind put their faith.

The vessel was turning over, compressed air or steam burst up the decks with loud reports; fragments of wreckage flew into the air. There the poor captain still clung to the rail of the bridge. Seymour could see his white face—the moonlight seemed to paint it with a ghastly smile. The officer in command of their boat shouted to the crew to give way lest they should be sucked down with the steamer.

Look! Now she wallowed like a dying whale, the moonrays shone white upon her bottom, showing the jagged rent made in it by the rock on which she had struck, and now she was gone. Only a little cloud of smoke and steam remained to mark where the *Zanzibar* had been.

III.
HOW ROBERT CAME ASHORE

In place of the *Zanzibar* a great pit on the face of the ocean, in which the waters boiled and black objects appeared and disappeared.

"Sit still, for your lives' sake," said the officer in a quiet voice; "the suck is coming."

In another minute it came, dragging them downward till the water trickled over the sides of the boat, and backward towards the pit. But before ever they reached it the deep had digested its prey, and, save for the great air-bubbles which burst about them and a mixed, unnatural swell, was calm again. For the moment they were safe.

"Passengers," said the officer, "I am going to put out to sea—at any rate, till daylight. We may meet a vessel there, and if we try to row ashore we shall certainly be swamped in the breakers."

No one objected; they seemed too stunned to speak, but Robert thought to himself that the man was wise. They began to move, but before they had gone a dozen yards something dark rose beside them. It was a piece of wreckage, and clinging to it a woman, who clasped a bundle to her breast. More, she was alive, for she began to cry to them to take her in.

"Save me and my child!" she cried. "For God's sake save me!"

Robert recognized the choking voice; it was that of a young married lady with whom he had been very friendly, who was going out with her baby to join her husband in Natal. He stretched out his hand and caught hold of her, whereon the officer said, heavily:

"The boat is already overladen. I must warn you that to take more aboard is not safe."

Thereon the passengers awoke from their stupor.

"Push her off," cried a voice; "she must take her chance." And there was a murmur of approval at the dreadful words.

"For Christ's sake—for Christ's sake!" wailed the drowning woman, who clung desperately to Robert's hand.

"If you try to pull her in, we will throw you overboard," said the voice again, and a knife was lifted as though to hack at his arm. Then the officer spoke once more.

"This lady cannot come into the boat unless someone goes out of it. I would myself, but it is my duty to stay. Is there any man here who will make place for her?"

But all the men there—seven of them, besides the crew—hung their heads and were silent.

"Give way," said the officer in the same heavy voice; "she will drop off presently."

While the words passed his lips Robert seemed to live a year. Here was an opportunity of atonement for his idle and luxurious life. An hour ago he would have taken it gladly, but now—now, with Benita senseless on his breast, and that answer still locked in her sleeping heart? Yet Benita would approve of such a death as this, and even if she loved him not in life, would learn to love his memory. In an instant his mind was made up, and he was speaking rapidly.

"Thompson," he said to the officer, "if I go, will you swear to take her in and her child?"

"Certainly, Mr. Seymour."

"Then lay to; I am going. If any of you live, tell this lady how I died," and he pointed to Benita, "and say I thought that she would wish it."

"She shall be told," said the officer again, "and saved, too, if I can do it."

"Hold Mrs. Jeffreys, then, till I am out of this. I'll leave my coat to cover her."

A sailor obeyed, and with difficulty Robert wrenched free his hand.

Very deliberately he pressed Benita to his breast and kissed her on the forehead, then let her gently slide on to the bottom of the boat. Next he slipped off his overcoat and slowly rolled himself over the gunwale into the sea.

"Now," he said, "pull Mrs. Jeffreys in."

"God bless you; you are a brave man," said Thompson. "I shall remember you if I live a hundred years."

But no one else said anything; perhaps they were all too much ashamed, even then.

"I have only done my duty," Seymour answered from the water. "How far is it to the shore?"

"About three miles," shouted Thompson. "But keep on that plank, or you will never live through the rollers. Good-bye."

"Good-bye," answered Robert.

Then the boat passed away from him and soon vanished in the misty face of the deep.

Resting on the plank which had saved the life of Mrs. Jeffreys, Robert Seymour looked about him and listened. Now and again he heard a faint, choking scream uttered by some drowning wretch, and a few hundred yards away caught sight of a black object which he thought might be a boat. If so, he reflected that it must be full. Moreover, he could not overtake it. No; his only chance was to make for the shore. He was a strong swimmer, and happily the water was almost as warm as milk. There seemed to be no reason why he should not reach it, supported as he was by a lifebelt, if the sharks would leave him alone, which they might, as there was plenty for them to feed on. The direction he knew well enough, for now in the great silence of the sea he could hear the boom of the mighty rollers breaking on the beach.

Ah, those rollers! He remembered how that very afternoon Benita and he had watched them through his field glass spouting up against the cruel walls of rock, and wondered that when the ocean was so calm they had still such power. Now, should he live to reach them, he was doomed to match himself against that power. Well, the sooner he did so the sooner it would be over, one way or the other. This was in his favour: the tide had turned, and was flowing shorewards. Indeed, he had little to do but to rest upon his plank, which he placed crosswise beneath his breast, and steered himself with his feet. Even thus he made good progress, nearly a mile an hour perhaps. He could have gone faster had he swum, but he was saving his strength.

It was a strange journey upon that silent sea beneath those silent stars, and strange thoughts came into Robert's soul. He wondered whether Benita would live and what she would say. Perhaps, however, she was already dead, and he would meet her presently. He wondered if he were doomed to die, and whether this sacrifice of his would be allowed to atone for his past errors. He hoped so, and put up a petition to that effect, for himself and for Benita, and for all the poor people who had gone before, hurled from their pleasure into the halls of Death.

So he floated on while the boom of the breakers grew ever nearer, companioned by his wild, fretful thoughts, till at length what he took to be a shark appeared quite close to him, and in the urgency of the moment he gave up wondering. It proved to be only a piece of wood, but later on a real shark did come, for he saw its back fin. However, this cruel creature was either gorged or timid, for when he splashed upon the water and shouted, it went away, to return no more.

Now, at length, Robert entered upon the deep hill and valley swell which preceded the field of the rollers. Suddenly he shot down a smooth slope, and without effort of his own found himself borne up an opposing steep, from the crest of which he had a view of white lines of foam, and beyond them of a dim and rocky shore. At one spot, a little to his right, the foam seemed thinner and the line of cliff to be broken, as though here there was a cleft. For this cleft, then, he steered his plank, taking the swell obliquely, which by good fortune the set of the tide enabled him to do without any great exertion.

The valleys grew deeper, and the tops of the opposing ridges were crested with foam. He had entered the rollers, and the struggle for life began. Before him they rushed solemn and mighty. Viewed from some safe place even the sight of these combers is terrible, as any who have watched them from this coast, or from that of the Island of Ascension, can bear witness. What their aspect was to this shipwrecked man, supported by a single plank, may therefore be imagined, seen, as he saw them, in the mysterious moonlight and in utter loneliness. Yet his spirit rose to meet the dread emergency; if he were to die, he would die fighting. He had grown cold and tired, but now the chill and weariness left him; he felt warm and strong. From the crest of one of the high rollers he thought he saw that about half a mile away from him a little river ran down the centre of the gorge, and for the mouth of this river he laid his course.

At first all went well. He was borne up the seas; he slid down the seas in a lather of white foam. Presently the rise and fall grew steeper, and the foam began to break over his head. Robert could no longer guide himself; he must go as he was carried. Then in an instant he was carried into a hell of waters where, had it not been for his lifebelt and the plank, he must have been beaten down and have perished. As it was, now he was driven into the depths, and now he emerged upon their surface to hear their seething hiss around him, and above it all a continuous boom as of great guns—the boom of the breaking seas.

The plank was almost twisted from his grasp, but he clung to it desperately, although its edges tore his arms. When the rollers broke over him he held his breath, and when he was tossed skywards on their curves, drew it again in quick, sweet gasps. Now he sat upon the very brow of one of them as a merman might; now he dived like a dolphin, and now, just as his senses were leaving him, his feet touched bottom. Another moment and Robert was being rolled along that bottom with a weight on him like the weight of mountains. The plank was rent from him, but his cork jacket brought him up. The backwash drew him with it into deeper water, where he lay helpless and despairing, for he no longer had any strength to struggle against his doom.

Then it was that there came a mighty roller, bigger than any that he had seen—such a one as on that coast the Kaffirs call "a father of waves." It caught him in the embrace of its vast green curve. It bore him forward as though he were but a straw, far forward over the stretch of cruel rocks. It broke in thunder, dashing him again upon the stones and sand of the little river bar, rolling him along with its resistless might, till even that might was exhausted, and its foam began to return seawards, sucking him with it.

Robert's mind was almost gone, but enough of it remained to tell him that if once more he was dragged into the deep water he must be lost. As the current haled him along he gripped at the bottom with his hands, and by the mercy of Heaven they closed on something. It may have been a tree-stump embedded there, or a rock—he never knew. At least, it was firm, and to it he hung despairingly. Would that rush never cease? His lungs were bursting; he must let go! Oh! the foam was thinning; his head was above it now; now it had departed, leaving him like a stranded fish upon the shingle. For half a minute or more he lay there gasping, then looked behind him to see another comber approaching through the gloom. He struggled to his feet, fell, rose again, and ran, or rather, staggered forward with that tigerish water hissing at his heels. Forward, still forward, till he was beyond its reach—yes, on dry sand. Then his vital forces failed him; one of his legs gave way, and, bleeding from a hundred hurts, he fell heavily onto his face, and there was still.

The boat in which Benita lay, being so deep in the water, proved very hard to row against the tide, for the number of its passengers encumbered the oarsmen. After a while a light off land breeze sprang up, as here it often does towards morning; and the officer, Thompson, determined to risk hoisting the sail. Accordingly this was done—with some difficulty, for the mast had to be drawn out and shipped—although the women screamed as the weight of the air bent their frail craft over till the gunwale was almost level with the water.

"Anyone who moves shall be thrown overboard!" said the officer, who steered, after which they were quiet.

Now they made good progress seawards, but the anxieties of those who knew were very great, since the wind showed signs of rising, and if any swell should spring up that crowded cutter could scarcely hope to live. In fact, two hours later they were forced to lower the sail again and drift, waiting for the dawn. Mr. Thompson strove to cheer them, saying that now they were in the track of vessels, and if they could see none when the light came, he would run along the shore in the hope of finding a place free of breakers where they might land. If they did not inspire hope, at least his words calmed them, and they sat in heavy silence, watching the sky.

At length it grew grey, and then, with a sudden glory peculiar to South Africa, the great red sun arose and began to dispel the mist from the surface of the sea. Half an hour more and this was gone, and now the bright rays brought life back into their chilled frames as they stared at each other to see which of their company were still left alive. They even asked for food, and biscuit was given to them with water.

All this while Benita remained unconscious. Indeed, one callous fellow, who had been using her body as a footstool, said that she must be dead, and had better be thrown overboard, as it would lighten the boat.

"If you throw that lady into the sea, living or dead," said Mr. Thompson, with an ominous lift of his eye, "you go with her, Mr. Batten. Remember who brought her here and how he died."

Then Mr. Batten held his peace, while Thompson stood up and scanned the wide expanse of sea. Presently he whispered to a sailor near him, who also stood up, looked, and nodded.

"That will be the other Line's intermediate boat," he said, and the passengers, craning their heads round, saw far away to the right a streak of smoke upon the horizon. Orders were given, a little corner of sail was hoisted, with a white cloth of some sort tied above it, and the oars were got out. Once more the cutter moved forward, bearing to the left in the hope of intercepting the steamer.

She came on with terrible swiftness, and they who had miles of water to cover, dared hoist no more sail in that breeze. In half an hour she was nearly opposite to them, and they were still far away. A little more sail was let out, driving them through the water at as quick a rate as they could venture to go. The steamer was passing three miles or so away, and black despair took hold of them. Now the resourceful Thompson, without apologies, undressed, and removing the white shirt that he had worn at the dance, bade a sailor to tie it to an oar and wave it to and fro.

Still the steamer went on, until presently they heard her siren going, and saw that she was putting about.

"She has seen us," said Thompson. "Thank God, all of you, for there is wind coming up. Pull down that sail; we shan't need it any more."

Half an hour later, with many precautions, for the wind he prophesied was already troubling the sea and sending little splashes of water over the stern of their deeply laden boat, they were fast to a line thrown from the deck of the three thousand ton steamer *Castle*, bound for Natal. Then, with a rattle, down came the accommodation ladder, and strong-armed men, standing on its grating, dragged them one by one from the death to which they had been so near. The last to be lifted up, except Thompson, was Benita, round whom it was necessary to reeve a rope.

"Any use?" asked the officer on the grating as he glanced at her quiet form.

"Can't say; I hope so," answered Thompson. "Call your doctor." And gently enough she was borne up the ship's side.

They wanted to cast off the boat, but Thompson remonstrated, and in the end that also was dragged to deck. Meanwhile the news had spread, and the awakened passengers of the *Castle*, clad in pyjamas, dressing-gowns, and even blankets, were crowding round the poor castaways or helping them to their cabins.

"I am a teetotaller," said second officer Thompson when he had made a brief report to the captain of the *Castle*, "but if anyone will stand me a whiskey and soda I shall be obliged to him."

IV.
MR. CLIFFORD

Although the shock of the blow she had received upon her head was sufficient to make her insensible for so many hours, Benita's injuries were not of a really serious nature, for as it happened the falling block, or whatever it may have been, had hit her forehead slantwise, and not full, to which accident she owed it that, although the skin was torn and the scalp bruised, her skull had escaped fracture. Under proper medical care her senses soon came back to her, but as she was quite dazed and thought herself still on board the *Zanzibar*, the doctor considered it wise to preserve her in that illusion for a while. So after she had swallowed some broth he gave her a sleeping draught, the effects of which she did not shake off till the following morning.

Then she came to herself completely, and was astonished to feel the pain in her head, which had been bandaged, and to see a strange stewardess sitting by her with a cup of beef-tea in her hand.

"Where am I? Is it a dream?" she asked.

"Drink this and I will tell you," answered the stewardess.

Benita obeyed, for she felt hungry, then repeated her question.

"Your steamer was shipwrecked," said the stewardess, "and a great many poor people were drowned, but you were saved in a boat. Look, there are your clothes; they were never in the water."

"Who carried me into the boat?" asked Benita in a low voice.

"A gentleman, they say, Miss, who had wrapped you in a blanket and put a lifebelt on you."

Now Benita remembered everything that happened before the darkness fell—the question to which she had given no answer, the young couple who stood flirting by her—all came back to her.

"Was Mr. Seymour saved?" she whispered, her face grey with dread.

"I dare say, Miss," answered the stewardess evasively. "But there is no gentleman of that name aboard this ship."

At that moment the doctor came in, and him, too, she plied with questions. But having learned the story of Robert's self-sacrifice from Mr. Thompson and the others, he would give her no answer, for he guessed how matters had stood between them, and feared the effects of the shock. All he could say was that he hoped Mr. Seymour had escaped in some other boat.

It was not until the third morning that Benita was allowed to learn the truth, which indeed it was impossible to conceal any longer. Mr. Thompson came to her cabin and told her everything, while she listened silently, horrified, amazed.

"Miss Clifford," he said, "I think it was one of the bravest things that a man ever did. On the ship I always thought him rather a head-in-air kind of swell, but he was a splendid fellow, and I pray God that he has lived, as the lady and child for whom he offered himself up have done, for they are both well again."

"Yes," she repeated after him mechanically, "splendid fellow indeed, and," she added, with a strange flash of conviction, "I believe that he *is* still alive. If he were dead I should know it."

"I am glad to hear you say so," said Mr. Thompson, who believed the exact contrary.

"Listen," she went on. "I will tell you something. When that dreadful accident occurred Mr. Seymour had just asked me to marry him, and I was going to answer that I would—because I love him. I believe that I shall still give him that answer."

Mr. Thompson replied again that he hoped so, which, being as honest and tender-hearted as he was brave and capable, he did most earnestly; but in his heart he reflected that her answer would not be given this side of the grave. Then, as he had been deputed to do, he handed her the note which had been found in the bosom of her dress, and, able to bear no more of this painful scene, hurried from the cabin. She read it greedily twice, and pressed it to her lips, murmuring:

"Yes, I will think kindly of you, Robert Seymour, kindly as woman can of man, and now or afterwards you shall have your answer, if you still wish for it. Whenever you come or wherever I go, it shall be ready for you."

That afternoon, when she was more composed, Mrs. Jeffreys came to see Benita, bringing her baby with her. The poor woman was still pale and shaken, but the child had taken no hurt at all from its immersion in that warm water.

"What can you think of me?" she said, falling on her knees by Benita. "But oh! I did not know what I was doing. It was terror and my child," and she kissed the sleeping infant passionately. "Also I did not understand at the time—I was too dazed. And—that hero—he gave his life for me when the others wished to beat me off with oars. Yes, his blood is upon my hands—he who died that I and my child might live."

Benita looked at her and answered, very gently:

"Perhaps he did not die after all. Do not grieve, for if he did it was a very glorious death, and I am prouder of him than I could have been had he lived on like the others—who wished to beat you off with oars. Whatever is, is by God's Will, and doubtless for the best. At the least, you and your child will be restored to your husband, though it cost me one who would have been—my husband."

That evening Benita came upon the deck and spoke with the other ladies who were saved, learning every detail that she could gather. But to none of the men, except to Mr. Thompson, would she say a single word, and soon, seeing how the matter stood, they hid themselves away from her as they had already done from Mrs. Jeffreys.

The *Castle* had hung about the scene of the shipwreck for thirty hours, and rescued one other boatload of survivors, also a stoker clinging to a piece of wreckage. But with the shore she had been unable to communicate, for the dreaded wind had risen, and the breakers were quite impassable to any boat. To a passing steamer bound for Port Elizabeth, however, she had reported the terrible disaster, which by now was known all over the world, together with the names of those whom she had picked up in the boats.

On the night of the day of Benita's interview with Mrs. Jeffreys, the *Castle* arrived off Durban and anchored, since she was too big a vessel to cross the bar as it was in those days. At dawn the stewardess awoke Benita from the uneasy sleep in which she lay, to tell her that an old gentleman had come off in the tug and wished to see her; for fear of exciting false hopes she was very careful to add that word "old."

With her help Benita dressed herself, and as the sun rose, flooding the Berea, the Point, the white town and fair Natal beyond with light, she went on to the deck, and there, leaning over the bulwark, saw a thin, grey-bearded man of whom after all these years the aspect was still familiar.

A curious thrill went through her as she looked at him leaning there lost in thought. After all, he was her father, the man to whom she owed her presence upon this bitter earth, this place of terrors and delights, of devastation and hope supernal. Perhaps, too, he had been as much sinned against as sinning. She stepped up to him and touched him on the shoulder.

"Father," she said.

He turned round with all the quickness of a young man, for about him there was a peculiar agility which his daughter had inherited. Like his mind, his body was still nimble.

"My darling," he said, "I should have known your voice anywhere. It has haunted my sleep for years. My darling, thank you for coming back to me, and thank God for preserving you when so many were lost." Then he threw his arms about her and kissed her.

She shrank from him a little, for by inadvertence he had pressed upon the wound in her forehead.

"Forgive me," she said; "it is my head. It was injured, you know."

Then he saw the bandage about her brow, and was very penitent.

"They did not tell me that you had been hurt, Benita," he exclaimed in his light, refined voice, one of the stamps of that gentility of blood and breeding whereof all his rough years and errors had been unable to deprive him. "They only told me that you were saved. It is part of my ill-fortune that at our first moment of greeting I should give you pain, who have caused you so much already."

Benita felt that the words were an apology for the past, and her heart was touched.

"It is nothing," she answered. "You did not know or mean it."

"No, dear, I never knew or meant it. Believe me, I was not a willing sinner, only a weak one. You are beautiful, Benita—far more so than I expected."

"What," she answered smiling, "with this bandage round my head? Well, in your eyes, perhaps." But inwardly she thought to herself that the description would be more applicable to her father, who in truth, notwithstanding his years, was wonderfully handsome, with his quick blue eyes, mobile face, gentle mouth with the wistful droop at the corners so like her own, and grey beard. How, she wondered, could this be the man who had struck her mother. Then she remembered him as he had been years before when he was a slave to liquor, and knew that the answer was simple.

"Tell me about your escape, love," he said, patting her hand with his thin fingers. "You don't know what I've suffered. I was waiting at the Royal Hotel here, when the cable came announcing the loss of the *Zanzibar* and all on board. For the first time for many a year I drank spirits to drown my grief—don't be afraid, dear—for the first time and the last. Then afterwards came another cable giving the names of those who were known to be saved, and—thank God, oh! thank God—yours among them," and he gasped at the recollection of that relief.

"Yes," she said; "I suppose I should thank—Him—and another. Have you heard the story about—how Mr. Seymour saved me, I mean?"

"Some of it. While you were dressing yourself, I have been talking to the officer who was in command of your boat. He was a brave man, Benita, and I am sorry to tell you he is gone."

She grasped a stanchion and clung there, staring at him with a wild, white face.

"How do you know that, Father?"

Mr. Clifford drew a copy of the *Natal Mercury* of the previous day from the pocket of his ulster, and while she waited in an agony he hunted through the long columns descriptive of the loss of the *Zanzibar*. Presently he came to the paragraph he sought, and read it aloud to her. It ran:

"The searchers on the coast opposite the scene of the shipwreck report that they met a Kaffir who was travelling along the seashore, who produced a gold watch which he said he had taken from the body of a white man that he found lying on the sand at the mouth of the Umvoli River. Inside the watch is engraved, 'To Seymour Robert

Seymour, from his uncle, on his twenty-first birthday.' The name of Mr. Seymour appears as a first-class passenger to Durban by the *Zanzibar*. He was a member of an old English family in Lincolnshire. This was his second journey to South Africa, which he visited some years ago with his brother on a big-game shooting expedition. All who knew him then will join with us in deploring his loss. Mr. Seymour was a noted shot and an English gentleman of the best stamp. He was last seen by one of the survivors of the catastrophe, carrying Miss Clifford, the daughter of the well-known Natal pioneer of that name, into a boat, but as this young lady is reported to have been saved, and as he entered the boat with her, no explanation is yet forthcoming as to how he came to his sad end."

"I fear that is clear enough," said Mr. Clifford, as he folded up his paper.

"Yes, clear enough," she repeated in a strained voice. "And yet—yet—oh! Father, he had just asked me to marry him, and I can't believe that he is dead before I had time to answer."

"Good Heavens!" said the old man, "they never told me that. It is dreadfully sad. God help you, my poor child! There is nothing more to say except that he was only one among three hundred who have gone with him. Be brave now, before all these people. Look—here comes the tug."

The following week was very much of a blank to Benita. When they reached shore some old friends of her father's took her and him to their house, a quiet place upon the Berea. Here, now that the first excitement of rescue and grief was over, the inevitable reaction set in, bringing with it weakness so distressing that the doctor insisted upon her going to bed, where she remained for the next five days. With the healing up of the wound in her head her strength came back to her at last, but it was a very sad Benita who crept from her room one afternoon on to the verandah and looked out at the cruel sea, peaceful now as the sky above.

Her father, who had nursed her tenderly during these dark days, came and sat by her, taking her hand in his.

"This is capital," he said, glancing at her anxiously. "You are getting quite yourself again."

"I shall never be myself again," she answered. "My old self is dead, although the outside of me has recovered. Father, I suppose that it is wrong, but I wish that I were dead too. I wish that he had taken me with him when he jumped into the sea to lighten the boat."

"Don't speak like that," he broke in hastily. "Of course I know that I am not much to you—how can I be after all that is past? But I love you, dear, and if I were left quite alone again——" And he broke off.

"You shall not be left alone if I can help it," she replied, looking at the old man with her dark and tender eyes. "We have only each other in the world now, have we? The rest have gone, never to return."

He threw his arms about her, and, drawing her to him, kissed her passionately.

"If only you could learn to love me!" he said.

"I do love you," she answered, "who now shall never love any other man upon the earth."

This was the beginning of a deep affection which sprang up between Mr. Clifford and his daughter, and continued to the end.

"Is there any news?" she asked a little later.

"None—none about him. The tide took his body away, no doubt, after the Kaffir had gone. I remember him well now. He was a fine young man, and it comes into my mind that when I said good-bye to him above those old ruins, I wished that I had a son like that. And to think that he went so near to becoming a son to me! Well, the grass must bend when the wind blows, as the natives say."

"I am glad that you knew him," she answered simply.

Then they began talking about other matters. He told her that all the story had become known, and that people spoke of Robert Seymour as "the hero"; also that there was a great deal of curiosity about her.

"Then let us get away as soon as we can," she said nervously. "But, Father, where are we going?"

"That will be for you to decide, love. Listen, now; this is my position. I have been quite steady for years, and worked hard, with the result that I and my partner have a fine farm in the Transvaal, on the high land near Lake Chrissie, out Wakkerstroom way. We breed horses there, and have done very well with them. I have £1,500 saved, and the farm brings us in quite £600 a year beyond the expenses. But it is a lonely place, with only a few Boers about, although they are good fellows enough. You might not care to live there with no company."

"I don't think that I should mind," she answered, smiling.

"Not now, but by-and-by you would when you know what it is like. Now I might sell my share in the farm to my partner, who, I think, would buy it, or I might trust to him to send me a part of the profits, which perhaps he would not. Then, if you wish it, we could live in or near one of the towns, or even, as you have an income of your own, go home to England, if that is your will."

"Is it your will?" she asked.

He shook his head. "No; all my life is here. Also, I have something to find before I die—for your sake, dear."

"Do you mean up among those ruins?" she asked, looking at him curiously.

"Yes. So you know about it?" he answered, with a flash of his blue eyes. "Oh! of course, Seymour told you. Yes, I mean among the ruins—but I will tell you that story another time—not here, not here. What do you wish to do, Benita? Remember, I am in your hands; I will obey you in all things."

"Not to stop in a town and not to go to England," she replied, while he hung eagerly upon her words, "for this has become my holy land. Father, I will go with you to your farm; there I can be quiet, you and I together."

"Yes," he answered rather uneasily; "but, you see, Benita, we shall not be quite alone there. My partner, Jacob Meyer, lives with me."

"Jacob Meyer? Ah! I remember," and she winced. "He is a German, is he not—and odd?"

"German Jew, I imagine, and very odd. Should have made his fortune a dozen times over, and yet has never done anything. Too unpractical, too visionary, with all his brains and scheming. Not a good man, Benita, although he suits me, and, for the matter of that, under our agreement I cannot get rid of him."

"How did he become your partner?" she asked.

"Oh! a good many years ago he turned up at the place with a doleful story. Said that he had been trading among the Zulus; he was what we call a 'smouse' out here, and got into a row with them, I don't know how. The end of it was that they burned his waggon, looted his trade-goods and oxen, and killed his servants. They would have killed him too, only, according to his own account, he escaped in a very queer fashion."

"How?"

"Well, he says by mesmerising the chief and making the man lead him through his followers. An odd story enough, but I can quite believe it of Jacob. He worked for me for six months, and showed himself very clever. Then one night, I remember it was a few days after I had told him of the story of the Portuguese treasure in Matabeleland, he produced £500 in Bank of England notes out of the lining of his waistcoat, and offered to buy a half interest in the farm. Yes, £500! Although for all those months I had believed him to be a beggar. Well, as he was so *slim*, and better than no company in that lonely place, in the end I accepted. We have done well since, except for the expedition after the treasure which we did not get, although we more than paid our expenses out of the ivory we bought. But next time we shall succeed, I am sure," he added with enthusiasm, "that is, if we can persuade those Makalanga to let us search on the mountain."

Benita smiled.

"I think you had better stick to the horsebreeding," she said.

"You shall judge when you hear the story. But you have been brought up in England; will you not be afraid to go to Lake Chrissie?"

"Afraid of what?" she asked.

"Oh! of the loneliness, and of Jacob Meyer."

"I was born on the veld, Father, and I have always hated London. As for your odd friend, Mr. Meyer, I am not afraid of any man on earth. I have done with men. At the least I will try the place and see how I get on."

"Very well," answered her father with a sigh of relief. "You can always come back, can't you?"

"Yes," she said indifferently. "I suppose that I can always come back."

V.
JACOB MEYER

More than three weeks had gone by when one morning Benita, who slept upon the cartel or hide-strung bed in the waggon, having dressed herself as best she could in that confined place, thrust aside the curtain and seated herself upon the voorkisse, or driving-box. The sun was not yet up, and the air was cold with frost, for they were on the Transvaal high-veld at the end of winter. Even through her thick cloak Benita shivered and called to the driver of the waggon, who also acted as cook, and whose blanket-draped form she could see bending over a fire into which he was blowing life, to make haste with the coffee.

"By and by, Missie—by and by," he answered, coughing the rank smoke from his lungs. "Kettle no sing yet, and fire black as hell."

Benita reflected that popular report painted this locality red, but without entering into argument sat still upon the chest waiting till the water boiled and her father appeared.

Presently he emerged from under the side flap of the waggon where he slept, and remarking that it was really too cold to think of washing, climbed to her side by help of the disselboom, and kissed her.

"How far are we now from Rooi Krantz, Father?" she asked, for that was the name of Mr. Clifford's farm.

"About forty miles, dear. The waggon cannot make it to-night with these two sick oxen, but after the midday outspan we will ride on, and be there by sundown. I am afraid you are tired of this trekking."

"No," she answered. "I like it very much; it is so restful, and I sleep sound upon that cartel. I feel as though I should like to trek on for the rest of my life."

"So you shall if you wish, dear, for whole months. South Africa is big, and when the grass grows, if you still wish it, we will take a long journey."

She smiled, but made no answer, knowing that he was thinking of the place so far away where he believed that once the Portuguese had buried gold.

The kettle was singing now merrily enough, and Hans, the cook, lifting it from the fire in triumph—for his blowing exertions had been severe—poured into it a quantity of ground coffee from an old mustard tin. Then, having stirred the mixture with a stick, he took a red ember from the fire and dropped it into the kettle, a process which, as travellers in the veld know well, has a clearing effect upon the coffee. Next he produced pannikins, and handed them up with a pickle jar full of sugar to Mr. Clifford, upon the waggon chest. Milk they had none, yet that coffee tasted a great deal better than it looked; indeed, Benita drank two cups of it to warm herself and wash down the hard biscuit. Before the day was over glad enough was she that she had done so.

The sun was rising; huge and red it looked seen through the clinging mist, and, their breakfast finished, Mr. Clifford gave orders that the oxen, which were filling themselves with the dry grass near at hand, should be got up and inspanned. The voorlooper, a Zulu boy, who had left them for a little while to share the rest of the coffee with Hans, rose from his haunches with a grunt, and departed to fetch them. A minute or two later Hans ceased from his occupation of packing up the things, and said in a low voice:

"*Kek!* Baas"—that is "Look!"

Following the line of his outstretched hand, Benita and her father perceived, not more than a hundred yards away from them, a great troop of wilderbeeste, or gnu, travelling along a ridge, and pausing now and again to indulge in those extraordinary gambols which cause the Boers to declare that these brutes have a worm in their brains.

"Give me my rifle, Hans," said Mr. Clifford. "We want meat."

By the time that the Westley-Richards was drawn from its case and loaded, only one buck remained, for, having caught sight of the waggon, it turned to stare at it suspiciously. Mr. Clifford aimed and fired. Down went the buck, then springing to its feet again, vanished behind the ridge. Mr. Clifford shook his head sadly.

"I don't often do that sort of thing, my dear, but the light is still very bad. Still, he's hit. What do you say? Shall we get on the horses and catch him? A canter would warm you."

Benita, who was tender-hearted, reflected that it would be kinder to put the poor creature out of its pain, and nodded her head. Five minutes later they were cantering together up the rise, Mr. Clifford having first ordered the waggon to trek on till they rejoined it, and slipped a packet of cartridges into his pocket. Beyond the rise lay a wide stretch of marshy ground, bordered by another rise half a mile or more away, from the crest of which—for now the air was clear enough—they saw the wounded bull standing. On they went after him, but before they could come within shot, he had moved forward once more, for he was only lightly hurt in the flank, and guessed whence his trouble came.

Again and again did he retreat as they drew near, until at length, just as Mr. Clifford was about to dismount to risk a long shot, the beast took to its heels in earnest.

"Come on," he said; "don't let's be beat," for by this time the hunter was alive in him.

So off they went at a gallop, up slopes and down slopes that reminded Benita of the Bay of Biscay in a storm, across half-dried vleis that in the wet season were ponds, through stony ground and patches of ant-bear holes in which they nearly came to grief. For five miles at least the chase went on, since at the end of winter the wilderbeeste was thin and could gallop well, notwithstanding its injury, faster even than their good horses. At last, rising a ridge, they found whither it was going, for suddenly they were in the midst of vast herds of game, thousands and tens of thousands of them stretching as far as the eye could reach.

It was a wondrous sight that now, alas! will be seen no more—at any rate upon the Transvaal veld; wilderbeeste, blesbok, springbok, in countless multitudes, and amongst them a few quagga and hartebeeste. With a sound like that of thunder, their flashing myriad hoofs casting up clouds of dust from the fire-blackened veld, the great herds separated at the appearance of their enemy, man. This way and that they went in groups and long brown lines, leaving the wounded and exhausted wilderbeeste behind them, so that presently he was the sole tenant of that great cup of land.

At him they rode till Mr. Clifford, who was a little ahead of his daughter, drew almost alongside. Then the poor maddened brute tried its last shift. Stopping suddenly, it wheeled round and charged head down. Mr. Clifford, as it came, held out his rifle in his right hand and fired at a hazard. The bullet passed through the bull, but could not stop its charge. Its horns, held low, struck the forelegs of the horse, and next instant horse, man, and wilderbeeste rolled on the veld together.

Benita, who was fifty yards behind, uttered a little cry of fear, but before ever she reached him, her father had risen laughing, for he was quite unhurt. The horse, too, was getting up, but the bull could rise no more. It struggled to its forefeet, uttered a kind of sobbing groan, stared round wildly, and rolled over, dead.

"I never knew a wilderbeeste charge like that before," said Mr. Clifford. "Confound it! I believe my horse is lamed."

Lamed it was, indeed, where the bull had struck the foreleg, though, as it chanced, not badly. Having tied a handkerchief to the horn of the buck in order to scare away the vultures, and thrown some tufts of dry grass upon its body, which he proposed, if possible, to fetch or send for, Mr. Clifford mounted his lame horse and headed for the waggon. But they had galloped farther than they thought, and it was midday before they came to what they took to be the road. As there was no spoor upon it, they followed this track backwards, expecting to find the waggon outspanned, but although they rode for mile upon mile, no waggon could they see. Then, realizing their mistake, they retraced their steps, and leaving this path at the spot where they had found it, struck off again to the right.

Meanwhile, the sky was darkening, and at about three o'clock in the afternoon a thunderstorm broke over them accompanied by torrents of icy rain, the first fall of the spring, and a bitter wind which chilled them through. More, after the heavy rain came drizzle and a thick mist that deepened as evening approached.

Now their plight was very wretched. Lost, starved, soaked to the skin, with tired horses one of which was lame, they wandered about on the lonely veld. Only one stroke of fortune came to them. As the sun set, for a few moments its rays pierced the mist, telling them in what direction they should go. Turning their horses, they headed for it, and so rode on until the darkness fell. Then they halted a while, but feeling that if they stood still in that horrible cold they would certainly perish before morning, once more pushed on again. By now Mr. Clifford's horse was almost too lame to ride, so he led it, walking at his daughter's side, and reproaching himself bitterly for his foolishness in having brought her into this trouble.

"It doesn't matter, Father," she answered wearily, for she was very tired. "Nothing matters; one may as well die upon the veld as in the sea or anywhere else."

On they plodded, they knew not whither. Benita fell asleep upon her saddle, and was awakened once by a hyena howling quite close to them, and once by her horse falling to its knees.

"What is the time?" she said at last.

Her father struck a match and looked at his watch. It was ten o'clock; they had been fifteen hours away from the waggon and without food. At intervals Mr. Clifford, who had remounted, fired his rifle. Now there was but one cartridge left, and having caught sight of his daughter's exhausted face by the light of the match, he fired this also, though in that desperate wilderness there was little hope of its bringing succour.

"Shall we stop or go on?" he asked.

"I do not care," she answered. "Only if I stop I think it will be for ever. Let us go on."

Now the rain had ceased, but the mist was as dense as before. Also they seemed to have got among bush, for wet leaves brushed their faces. Utterly exhausted they stumbled forward, till suddenly Benita felt her horse stop as though a hand had seized its bridle, and heard a man's voice, speaking with a foreign accent, say:

"Mein Gott! Where are you going?"

"I wish I knew," she answered, like one in a dream.

At this instant the moon rose above the mists, and Benita saw Jacob Meyer for the first time.

In that light his appearance was not unpleasing. A man of about forty years of age, not over tall, slight and active in build, with a pointed black beard, regular, Semitic features, a complexion of an ivory pallor which even the African sun did not seem to tan, and dark, lustrous eyes that appeared, now to sleep, and now to catch the fire of the thoughts within. Yet, weary though she was, there was something in the man's personality which repelled and alarmed Benita, something wild and cruel. She felt that he was filled with unsatisfied ambitions and desires, and that to attain to them he would shrink at nothing. In a moment he was speaking again in tones that compelled her attention.

"It was a good thought that brought me here to look for you. No; not a thought—what do you call it?—an instinct. I think your mind must have spoken to my mind, and called me to save you. See now, Clifford, my friend, where you have led your daughter. See, see!" And he pointed downwards.

They leaned forward and stared. There, immediately beneath them, was a mighty gulf whereof the moonlight did not reveal the bottom.

"You are no good veld traveller, Clifford, my friend; one more step of those silly beasts, and down below there would have been two red heaps with bits of bones sticking out of them—yes, there on the rocks five hundred feet beneath. Ah! you would have slept soundly to-night, both of you."

"Where is the place?" asked Mr. Clifford in a dazed fashion. "Leopard's Kloof?"

"Yes; Leopard's Kloof, no other. You have travelled along the top of the hill, not at the bottom. Certainly that was a good thought which came to me from the lady your daughter, for she is one of the thought senders, I am sure. Ah! it came to me suddenly; it hit me like a stick whilst I was searching for you, having found that you had lost the waggon. It said to me, 'Ride to the top of Leopard's Kloof. Ride hard.' I rode hard through the rocks and the darkness, through the mist and the rain, and not one minute had I been here when you came and I caught the lady's bridle."

"I am sure we are very grateful to you," murmured Benita.

"Then I am paid back ten thousand times. No; it is I who am grateful—I who have saved your life through the thought you sent me."

"Thought or no thought, all's well that ends well," broke in Mr. Clifford impatiently. "And thank Heaven we are not more than three miles away from home. Will you lead the way, Jacob? You always could see in the dark?"

"Yes, yes," and he took hold of Benita's bridle with his firm, white hand. "Oh! my horse will follow, or put your arm through his rein—so. Now come on, Miss Clifford, and be afraid no more. With Jacob Meyer you are safe."

So they began their descent of the hill. Meyer did not speak again; all his attention seemed to be concentrated upon finding a safe path on which the horses would not stumble. Nor did Benita speak; she was too utterly exhausted—so exhausted, indeed, that she could no longer control her mind and imagination. These seemed to loose themselves from her and to acquire new powers, notably that of entering into the secret thoughts of the man at her side. She saw them pass before her like living things, and yet she could not read them. Still, something she did understand—that she had suddenly grown important to this man, not in the way in which women are generally important to men, but otherwise. She felt as though she had become interwoven with the objects of his life, and was henceforth necessary to their fulfilment, as though she were someone whom he had been seeking for years on years, the one person who could give him light in his darkness.

These imaginings troubled her, so that she was very thankful when they passed away as swiftly as they had arisen, and she knew only that she was half dead with weariness and cold; that her limbs ached and that the steep path seemed endless.

At length they reached level ground, and after travelling along it for a while and crossing the bed of a stream, passed through a gate, and stopped suddenly at the door of a house with lighted windows.

"Here is your home at last, Miss Clifford," said the musical voice of Jacob Meyer, "and I thank the Fate which rules us that it has taught me to bring you to it safely."

Making no answer she slid from the saddle, only to find that she could not stand, for she sank into a heap upon the ground. With a gentle exclamation he lifted her, and calling to two Kaffirs who had appeared to take the horses, led her into the house.

"You must go to bed at once," he said, conducting her to a door which opened out of the sitting-room. "I have had a fire lit in your chamber in case you should come, and old Tante Sally will bring you soup with brandy in it, and hot water for your feet. Ah! there you are, old vrouw. Come now; help the lady, your mistress. Is all ready?"

"All, Baas," answered the woman, a stout half-breed with a kindly face. "Come now, my little one, and I will undress you."

Half an hour later Benita, having drunk more brandy than ever she had done in her life before, was wrapped up and fast asleep.

When she awoke the sun was streaming through the curtained window of her room, and by the light of it she saw that the clock which stood upon the mantelpiece pointed to half-past eleven. She had slept for nearly twelve hours, and felt that, notwithstanding the cold and exposure, save for stiffness and a certain numb feeling in her head—the result, perhaps, of the unaccustomed brandy—she was well and, what was more, quite hungry.

Outside on the verandah she heard the voice of Jacob Meyer, with which she seemed already to have become familiar, telling some natives to stop singing, as they would wake the chieftainess inside. He used the Zulu word Inkosi-kaas, which, she remembered, meant head-lady or chieftainess. He was very thoughtful for her, she reflected, and was grateful, till suddenly she remembered the dislike she had taken to the man.

Then she looked round her room and saw that it was very pretty, well furnished and papered, with water-colour pictures on the walls of no mean merit, things that she had not expected in this far-off place. Also on a table stood a great bowl of arum lilies. She wondered who had put them there; whether it were the old half-breed, Sally, or Jacob Meyer. Also she wondered who had painted the pictures, which were all of African scenery, and something told her that both the flowers and the pictures came from Jacob Meyer.

On the little table by her bed was a handbell, which presently she rang. Instantly she heard the voice of Sally calling for the coffee "quick," and next minute the woman entered, bringing a tray with it, and bread and butter—yes, and toast and eggs, which had evidently been made ready for her. Speaking in English mixed with Dutch words, she told Benita that her father was still in bed, but sent her his love, and wished to know how she did. Then, while she ate her breakfast with appetite, Sally set her a bath, and subsequently appeared carrying the contents of the box she had used upon the waggon, which had now arrived safely at the farm. Benita asked who had ordered the box to be unpacked, and Sally answered that the Heer Meyer had ordered it so that she might not be disturbed in her sleep, and that her things should be ready for her when she woke.

"The Heer Meyer thinks a great deal about other people," said Benita.

"Ja, ja!" answered the old half-breed. "He tink much about people when he want to tink about them, but he tink most about himself. Baas Meyer, he a very clever man—oh! a very clever man, who want to be a great man too. And one day, Missee, he be a great man, great and rich—if the Heer God Almighty let him."

VI.
THE GOLD COIN

Six weeks had gone by since the eventful evening of Benita's arrival at Rooi Krantz. Now the spring had fully come, the veld was emerald with grass and bright with flowers. In the kloof behind the house trees had put out their leaves, and the mimosas were in bloom, making the air heavy with their scent. Amongst them the ringdoves nested in hundreds, and on the steep rocks of the precipice the red-necked vultures fed their young. Along the banks of the stream and round the borders of the lake the pig-lilies bloomed, a sheet of white. All the place was beautiful and full of life and hope. Nothing seemed dead and hopeless except Benita's heart.

Her health had quite come back to her; indeed, never before had she felt so strong and well. But the very soul had withered in her breast. All day she thought, and all night she dreamed of the man who, in cold blood, had offered up his life to save a helpless woman and her child. She wondered whether he would have done this if he had heard the answer that was upon her lips. Perhaps that was why she had not been given time to speak that answer, which might have made a coward of him. For nothing more had been heard of Robert Seymour; indeed, already the tragedy of the ship *Zanzibar* was forgotten. The dead had buried their dead, and since then worse disasters had happened in the world.

But Benita could not bury her dead. She rode about the veld, she sat by the lake and watched the wild fowl, or at night heard them flighting over her in flocks. She listened to the cooing of the doves, the booming of the bitterns in the reeds, and the drumming of the snipe high in air. She counted the game trekking along the ridge till her mind grew weary. She sought consolation from the breast of Nature and found none; she sought it in the starlit skies, and oh! they were very far away. Death reigned within her who outwardly was so fair to see.

In the society of her father, indeed, she took pleasure, for he loved her, and love comforted her wounded heart. In that of Jacob Meyer also she found interest, for now her first fear of the man had died away, and undoubtedly he was very interesting; well-bred also after a fashion, although a Jew who had lost his own faith and rejected that of the Christians.

He told her that he was a German by birth, that he had been sent to England as a boy, to avoid the conscription, which Jews dislike, since in soldiering there is little profit. Here he had become a clerk in a house of South African merchants, and, as a consequence—having shown all the ability of his race—was despatched to take charge of a branch business in Cape Colony. What happened to him there Benita never discovered, but probably he had shown too much ability of an oblique nature. At any rate, his connection with the firm terminated, and for years he became a wandering "smouse," or trader, until at length he drifted into partnership with her father.

Whatever might have been his past, however, soon she found that he was an extremely able and agreeable man. It was he and no other who had painted the water-colours that adorned her room, and he could play and sing as well as he painted. Also, as Robert had told her, Mr. Meyer was very well-read in subjects that are not usually studied on the veld of South Africa; indeed, he had quite a library of books, most of them histories or philosophical and scientific works, of which he would lend her volumes. Fiction, however, he never read, for the reason, he told her, that he found life itself and the mysteries and problems which surround it so much more interesting.

One evening, when they were walking together by the lake, watching the long lights of sunset break and quiver upon its surface, Benita's curiosity overcame her, and she asked him boldly how it happened that such a man as he was content to live the life he did.

"In order that I may reach a better," he answered. "Oh! no, not in the skies, Miss Clifford, for of them I know nothing, nor, as I believe, is there anything to know. But here—here."

"What do you mean by a better life, Mr. Meyer?"

"I mean," he answered, with a flash of his dark eyes, "great wealth, and the power that wealth brings. Ah! I see you think me very sordid and materialistic, but money is God in this world, Miss Clifford—money is God."

She smiled and answered: "I fear, then, that he is likely to prove an invisible god on the high veld, Mr. Meyer. You will scarcely make a great fortune out of horse-breeding, and here there is no one to rule."

"Do you suppose, then, that is why I stop at Rooi Krantz, just to breed horses? Has not your father told you about the great treasure hidden away up there among the Makalanga?"

"I have heard something of it," she answered with a sigh. "Also that both of you went to look for it and were disappointed."

"Ah! The Englishman who was drowned—Mr. Seymour—he spoke of it, did he not? He found us there."

"Yes; and you wished to shoot him—do you remember?"

"God in Heaven! Yes, because I thought he had come to rob us. Well, I did not shoot, and afterwards we were hunted out of the place, which does not much matter, as those fools of natives refused to let us dig in the fortress."

"Then why do you still think about this treasure which probably does not exist?"

"Why, Miss Clifford, do you think about various things that probably do not exist? Perhaps because you feel that here or elsewhere they *do* exist. Well, that is what I feel about the treasure, and what I have always felt. It exists, and I shall find it—now. I shall live to see more gold than you can even imagine, and that is why I still continue to breed horses on the Transvaal veld. Ah! you laugh; you think it is a nightmare that I breed——"

Then suddenly he became aware of Sally, who had appeared over the fold of the rise behind them, and asked irritably:

"What is it now, old vrouw?"

"The Baas Clifford wants to speak with you, Baas Jacob. Messengers have come to you from far away."

"What messengers?" he asked.

"I know not," answered Sally, fanning her fat face with a yellow pocket-handkerchief. "They are strange people to me, and thin with travelling, but they talk a kind of Zulu. The Baas wishes you to come."

"Will you come also, Miss Clifford? No? Then forgive me if I leave you," and lifting his hat he went.

"A strange man, Missee," said old Sally, when he had vanished, walking very fast.

"Yes," answered Benita, in an indifferent voice.

"A very strange man," went on the old woman. "Too much in his kop," and she tapped her forehead. "I tink it will burst one day; but if it does not burst, then he will be great. I tell you that before, now I tell it you again, for I tink his time come. Now I go cook dinner."

Benita sat by the lake till the twilight fell, and the wild geese began to flight over her. Then she walked back to the house thinking no more of Heer Meyer, thinking only that she was weary of this place in which there was nothing to occupy her mind and distract it from its ever present sorrow.

At dinner, or rather supper, that night she noticed that both her father and his partner seemed to be suffering from suppressed excitement, of which she thought she could guess the cause.

"Did you find your messengers, Mr. Meyer?" she asked, when the men had lit their pipes, and the square-face—as Hollands was called in those days, from the shape of the bottle—was set upon the rough table of speckled buchenhout wood.

"Yes, I found them," he answered; "they are in the kitchen now." And he looked at Mr. Clifford.

"Benita, my dear," said her father, "rather a curious thing has happened." Her face lit up, but he shook his head. "No, nothing to do with the shipwreck—that is all finished. Still, something that may interest you, if you care to hear a story."

Benita nodded; she was in a mood to hear anything that would occupy her thoughts.

"You know something about this treasure business," went on her father. "Well, this is the tale of it. Years ago, after you and your mother had gone to England, I went on a big game shooting expedition into the interior. My companion was an old fellow called Tom Jackson, a rolling stone, and one of the best elephant hunters in Africa. We did pretty well, but the end of it was that we separated north of the Transvaal, I bringing down the ivory that we had shot, and traded, and Tom stopping to put in another season, the arrangement being that he was to join me afterwards, and take his share of the money. I came here and bought this farm from a Boer who was tired of it—cheap enough, too, for I only gave him £100 for the 6,000 acres. The kitchens behind were his old house, for I built a new one.

"A year had gone by before I saw any more of Tom Jackson, and then he turned up more dead than alive. He had been injured by an elephant, and lay for some months among the Makalanga to the north of Matabeleland, where he got fever badly at a place called Bambatse, on the Zambesi. These Makalanga are a strange folk. I believe their name means the People of the Sun; at any rate, they are the last of some ancient race. Well, while he was there he cured the old Molimo, or hereditary high-priest of this tribe, of a bad fever by giving him quinine, and naturally they grew friendly. The Molimo lived among ruins of which there are many over all that part of South Africa. No one knows who built them now; probably it was people who lived thousands of years ago. However, this Molimo told Tom Jackson a more recent legend connected with the place.

"He said that six generations before, when his great-great-great grandfather was chief (Mambo, he called it), the natives of all that part of South Africa rose against the white men—Portuguese, I suppose—who still worked the gold there. They massacred them and their slaves by thousands, driving them up from the southward, where Lobengula rules now, to the Zambesi by which the Portuguese hoped to escape to the coast. At length a remnant of them, not more than about two hundred men and women, arrived at the stronghold called Bambatse, where the Molimo now lives in a great ruin built by the ancients upon an impregnable mountain which overhangs the river. With them they brought an enormous quantity of gold, all the stored-up treasure of the land which they were trying to carry off. But although they reached the river they could not escape by it, since the natives, who pursued them in thousands, watched day and night in canoes, and the poor fugitives had no boats. Therefore it came about that they were shut up in this fortress which it was impossible to storm, and there slowly perished of starvation.

"When it was known that they were all dead, the natives who had followed them from the south, and who wanted blood and revenge, not gold, which was of no use to them, went away; but the old priest's forefather who knew the secret entrance to the place, and who had been friendly to the Portuguese, forced his way in and there, amidst the dead, found one woman living, but mad with grief—a young and beautiful girl, the daughter of the Portuguese lord or captain. He gave her food, but in the night, when some strength had returned to her, she left him, and at daybreak he found her standing on the peak that overhangs the river, dressed all in white.

"He called some of his councillors, and they tried to persuade her to come down from the rock, but she answered, 'No, her betrothed and all her family and friends were dead, and it was her will to follow them.' Then they asked where was the gold, for having watched day and night they knew it had not been thrown into the river. She answered that it was where it was, and that, seek as he might, no black man would ever find it. She added that she gave it into his keeping, and that of his descendants, to safeguard until she came again. Also she said that if they were faithless to that trust, then it had been revealed to her from heaven above that those same savages who had killed her father and her people, would kill his people also. When she had spoken thus she stood a while praying on the peak, then suddenly hurled herself into the river, and was seen no more.

"From that day to this the ruin has been held to be haunted, and save the Molimo himself, who retires there to meditate and receive revelations from the spirits, no one is allowed to set a foot in its upper part; indeed, the natives would rather die than do so. Consequently the gold still remains where it was hidden. This place itself Tom Jackson did not see, since, notwithstanding his friendship for him, the Molimo refused to allow him to enter there.

"Well, Tom never recovered; he died here, and is buried in the little graveyard behind the house which the Boers made for some of their people. It was shortly before his death that Mr. Meyer became my partner, for I forgot to say that I had told him the story, and we determined to have a try for that great wealth. You know the rest. We trekked to Bambatse, pretending to be traders, and found the old Molimo who knew of me as having been Tom Jackson's friend. We asked him if the story he had told to Jackson were true, and he answered that, surely as the sun shone in the heavens, it was true— every word of it—for it, and much more than he had spoken of, had been handed down from father to son, and that they even knew the name of the white lady who had killed herself. It was Ferreira—your mother's name, Benita, though a common one enough in South Africa.

"We asked him to allow us to enter the topmost stronghold, which stands upon the hill, but he refused, saying that the curse still lay upon him and his, and that no man should enter until the lady Ferreira came again. For the rest the place was free to us; we might dig as we would. So we did dig, and found some gold buried with the ancients, beads and bangles and wire—about £100 worth. Also— that was on the day when the young Seymours came upon us, and accounts for Meyer's excitement, for he thought that we were on the track of the treasure—we found a single gold coin, no doubt one that had been dropped by the Portuguese. Here it is." And he threw a thin piece of gold on the table before her. "I have shown it to a man learned in those matters, and he says that it is a ducat struck by one of the doges of Venice.

"Well, we never found any more. The end of it was that the Makalanga caught us trying to get in to the secret stronghold by stealth, and gave us the choice of clearing out or being killed. So we cleared out, for treasure is not of much use to dead men."

Mr. Clifford ceased speaking, and filled his pipe, while Meyer helped himself to squareface in an absent manner. As for Benita, she stared at the quaint old coin, which had a hole in it, wondering with what scenes of terror and of bloodshed it had been connected.

"Keep it," said her father. "It will go on that bracelet of yours."

"Thank you, dear," she answered. "Though I don't know why I should take all the Portuguese treasure since we shall never see any more of it."

"Why not, Miss Clifford?" asked Meyer quickly.

"The story tells you why—because the natives won't even let you look for it; also, looking and finding are different things."

"Natives change their minds sometimes, Miss Clifford. That story is not done, it is only begun, and now you shall hear its second chapter. Clifford, may I call in the messengers?" And without waiting for an answer he rose and left the room.

Neither Mr. Clifford nor his daughter said anything after he had gone. Benita appeared to occupy herself in fixing the broad gold coin to a little swivel on her bracelet, but while she did so once more that sixth sense of hers awoke within her. As she had been afraid at the dinner on the doomed steamer, so again she was afraid. Again death and great fear cast their advancing shadows on to her soul. That piece of gold seemed to speak to her, yet, alas! she could not understand its story. Only she knew that her father and Jacob Meyer and—yes, yes, yes—Robert Seymour, had all a part in that tragedy. Oh! how could that be when he was dead? How could this gold link him to her? She knew not—she cared not. All she knew was that she would follow this treasure to the edge of the world, and if need be, over it, if only it brought her back to him again.

VII.
THE MESSENGERS

The door opened, and through it came Jacob Meyer, followed by three natives. Benita did not see or hear them; her soul was far away. There at the head of the room, clad all in white, for she wore no mourning save in her heart, illuminated by the rays of the lamp that hung above her, she stood still and upright, for she had risen; on the face and in her wide, dark eyes a look that was very strange to see. Jacob Meyer perceived it and stopped; the three natives perceived it also and stopped. There they stood, all four of them, at the end of the long sitting-room, staring at the white Benita and at her haunted eyes.

One of the natives pointed with his thin finger to her face, and whispered to the others. Meyer, who understood their tongue, caught the whisper. It was:

"Behold the Spirit of the Rock!"

"What spirit, and what rock?" he asked in a low voice.

"She who haunts Bambatse; she whom our eyes have seen," answered the man, still staring at Benita.

Benita heard the whispering, and knew it was about herself, though not one word of it did she catch. With a sigh she shook herself free from her visions and sat down in a chair close by. Then one by one the messengers drew near to her, and each, as he came, made a profound obeisance, touching the floor with his finger-tips, and staring at her face. But her father they only saluted with an uplifted hand. She looked at them with interest, and indeed they were interesting in their way; tall, spare men, light coloured, with refined, mobile faces. Here was no negro-blood, but rather that of some ancient people such as Egyptians or Phoenicians: men whose forefathers had been wise and civilized thousands of years ago, and perchance had stood in the courts of Pharaoh or of Solomon.

Their salutations finished, the three men squatted in a line upon the floor, drawing their fur karosses, or robes, about them, and waited in silence. Jacob Meyer thought a while, then said:

"Clifford, will you translate to your daughter, so that she may be sure she is told exactly what passes?"

Next he turned and addressed the natives.

"Your names are Tamas, Tamala, and Hoba, and you, Tamas, are the son of the Molimo of Bambatse, who is called Mambo, and you, Tamala and Hoba, are his initiated councillors. Is it so?"

They bowed their heads.

"Good. You, Tamas, tell the story and give again your message that this lady, the lady Benita, may hear it, for she has a part in the matter."

"We understand that she has a part," answered Tamas. "We read in her face that she has the greatest part. Doubtless it is of her that the Spirit told my father. These, spoken by my mouth, are the words of the Molimo, my father, which we have travelled so far to deliver.

"'When you two white men visited Bambatse four years ago, you asked of me, Mambo, to be admitted to the holy place, that you might look for the treasure there which the Portuguese hid in the time of my ancestor in the sixth generation. I refused to allow you to look, or even to enter the holy place, because I am by birth the guardian of that treasure, although I know not where it lies. But now I am in a great strait. I have news that Lobengula the usurper, who is king of the Matabele, has taken offence against me for certain reasons, among them that I did not send him a sufficient tribute. It is reported to me that he purposes next summer to despatch an impi to wipe me and my people out, and to make my kraal black as the burnt veld. I have little strength to resist him who is mighty, and my people are not warlike. From generation to generation they have been traders, cultivators of the land, workers in metal, and men of peace, who desire not to kill or be killed. Also they are few. Therefore I have no power to stand against Lobengula.

"'I remember the guns that you and your companion brought with you, which can kill things from far away. If I had a supply of those guns from behind my walls I might defy the impi of Lobengula, whose warriors use the assegai. If you will bring me a hundred good guns and plenty of powder and bullets for them, it is revealed to me that it will be lawful for me to admit you to the secret, holy place, where you may look for the buried gold for as long as you wish, and if you can find it, take it all away without hindrance from me or my people. But I will be honest with you. That gold will never be found save by the one appointed. The white lady said so in the time of my forefather; he heard it with his ears, and I have heard it from his descendants with my ears, and so it shall be. Still, if you bring the guns you can come and see if either of you is that one appointed. But I do not think that any man is so appointed, for the secret is hid in woman. But of this you can learn for yourselves. I do but speak as I am bidden.

"'This is my message spoken by my mouth, Tamas, son of my body, and my councillors who go with him will bear witness that he speaks the truth. I, Mambo, the Molimo of Bambatse, send you greeting, and will give you good welcome and fulfil my promise, if you come with the far-shooting guns, ten times ten of them, and the powder, and the bullets wherewith I may drive off the Matabele, but not otherwise. My son, Tamas, and my councillors will drive your waggon into my country but you must bring no strange servants. The Spirit of the white woman who killed herself before the eyes of my forefather has been seen of late standing upon the point of rock; also she has visited me at night in my secret place where her companions died. I do not know all that this portends, but I think that amongst other things she wished to tell me that the Matabele are about to attack us. I await the decree of the Heavens. I send you two karosses as a gift, and a little ancient gold, since ivory is too heavy for my messengers to carry, and I have no waggon. Farewell.'"

"We have heard you," said Meyer, when Mr. Clifford had finished translating, "and we wish to ask you a question. What do you mean when you say that the Spirit of the white woman has been seen?"

"I mean what I say, white man," answered Tamas. "She was seen by all three of us, standing upon the pinnacle at the dawn; also my father saw and spoke with her alone in his sleep at night. This is the third time in my father's day that she has appeared thus, and always before some great event."

"What was she like?" asked Meyer.

"Like? Oh! like the lady who sits yonder. Yes, quite the same, or so it seemed to us. But who knows? We have seen no other white women, and we were not very near. Let the lady come and stand side by side with the Spirit, so that we can examine them both, and we shall be able to answer better. Do you accept the offer of the Molimo?"

"We will tell you to-morrow morning," replied Meyer. "A hundred rifles are many to find, and will cost much money. Meanwhile, for you there is food and a sleeping-place."

The three men seemed disappointed at his answer, which they evidently believed to be preliminary to a refusal. For a moment or two they consulted together, then Tamas put his hand into a pouch and drew from it something wrapped in dry leaves, which he undid, revealing a quaint and beautiful necklace, fashioned of twisted gold links, wherein were set white stones, that they had no difficulty in recognising as uncut diamonds of considerable value. From this necklace also hung a crucifix moulded in gold.

"We offer this gift," he said, "on behalf of Mambo, my father, to the lady yonder, to whom the karosses and the rough gold are of no use. The chain has a story. When the Portuguese lady hurled herself into the river she wore it about her neck. As she fell into the river she struck against a little point of rock which tore the chain away from her—see where it is broken and mended with gold wire. It remained upon the point of rock, and my forefather took it thence. It is a gift to the lady if she will promise to wear it."

"Accept it," muttered Mr. Clifford, when he had finished translating this, "or you will give offence."

So Benita said: "I thank the Molimo, and accept his gift."

Then Tamas rose, and, advancing, cast the ancient, tragic thing over her head. As it fell upon her shoulders, Benita knew that it was a chain of destiny drawing her she knew not where, this ornament that had last been worn by that woman, bereaved and unhappy as herself, who could find no refuge from her sorrow except in death. Had she felt it torn from her breast, she wondered, as she, the living Benita of to-day, felt it fall upon her own?

The three envoys rose, bowed, and went, leaving them alone. Jacob Meyer lifted his head as though to address her, then changed his mind and was silent. Both the men waited for her to speak, but she would not, and in the end it was her father who spoke first.

"What do you say, Benita?" he asked anxiously.

"I? I have nothing to say, except that I have heard a very curious story. This priest's message is to you and Mr. Meyer, father, and must be answered by you. What have I to do with it?"

"A great deal, I think, my dear, or so those men seemed to believe. At any rate, I cannot go up there without you, and I will not take you there against your wish, for it is a long way off, and a queer business. The question is, will you go?"

She thought a space, while the two men watched her anxiously.

"Yes," she answered at length, in a quiet voice. "I will go if you wish to go, not because I want to find treasure, but because the story and the country where it happened interest me. Indeed, I don't believe much in the treasure. Even if they are superstitious and afraid to look for it themselves, I doubt whether they would allow you to look if they thought it could be found. To me the journey does not seem a good business speculation, also there are risks."

"We think it good enough," broke in Meyer decidedly. "And one does not expect to get millions without trouble."

"Yes, yes," said her father; "but she is right—there are risks, great risks—fever, wild beasts, savages, and others that one cannot foresee. Have I a right to expose her to them? Ought we not to go alone?"

"It would be useless," answered Meyer. "Those messengers have seen your daughter, and mixed her up with their superstitious story of a ghost, of which I, who know that there are no such things, believe nothing. Without her now we shall certainly fail."

"As for the risks, father," said Benita, "personally I take no account of them, for I am sure that what is to happen will happen, and if I knew that I was to die upon the Zambesi, it would make no difference to me who do not care. But as it chances, I think—I cannot tell you why—that you and Mr. Meyer are in more danger than I am. It is for you to consider whether you will take the risks."

Mr. Clifford smiled. "I am old," he said; "that is my answer."

"And I am accustomed to such things," said Meyer, with a shrug of his shoulders. "Who would not run a little danger for the sake of such a glorious chance? Wealth, wealth, more wealth than we can dream of, and with it, power—power to avenge, to reward, to buy position, and pleasure, and all beautiful things which are the heritage of the very rich alone," and he spread out his hands and looked upwards, as though in adoration of this golden god.

"Except such trifles as health and happiness," commented Benita, not without sarcasm, for this man and his material desires disgusted her somewhat, especially when she contrasted him with another man who was lost to her, though it was true that *his* past had been idle and unproductive enough. Yet they interested her also, for Benita had never met anyone like Mr. Meyer, so talented, so eager, and so soulless.

"Then I understand it is settled?" she said.

Mr. Clifford hesitated, but Meyer answered at once:

"Yes, settled as far as anything can be."

She waited a moment for her father to speak, but he said nothing; his chance had gone by.

"Very well. Now we shall not need to trouble ourselves with further doubts or argument. We are going to Bambatse on the Zambesi, a distant place, to look for buried gold, and I hope, Mr. Meyer, that if you find it, the results will come up to your expectations, and bring you all sorts of good luck. Good-night, father dear, good-night."

"My daughter thinks it will bring us ill-luck," said Mr. Clifford, when the door had closed behind her. "That is her way of saying so."

"Yes," answered Meyer gloomily; "she thinks that, and she is one of those who have vision. Well, she may be wrong. Also, the question is, shall we seize our opportunity and its dangers, or remain here and breed bad horses all our lives, while she who is not afraid laughs at us? I am going to Bambatse."

Again Mr. Clifford made no direct answer, only asked a question:

"How long will it take to get the guns and ammunition, and what will they cost?"

"About a week from Wakkerstroom," replied Meyer. "Old Potgieter, the trader there, has just imported a hundred Martinis and a hundred Westley-Richards falling-blocks. Fifty of each, with ten thousand rounds of cartridges, will cost about £600, and we have as much as that in the bank; also we have the new waggon, and plenty of good oxen and horses. We can take a dozen of the horses with us, and sell them in the north of the Transvaal for a fine price, before we get into the tetsefly belt. The oxen will probably carry us through, as they are most of them salted."

"You have thought it all out, Jacob, I see; but it means a lot of money one way and another, to say nothing of other things."

"Yes, a lot of money, and those rifles are too good for Kaffirs. Birmingham gas-pipes would have done for them, but there are none to be had. But what is the money, and what are the guns, compared to all they will bring us?"

"I think you had better ask my daughter, Jacob. She seems to have her own ideas upon the subject."

"Miss Clifford has made up her mind, and it will not change. I shall ask her no more," replied Meyer.

Then he, too, left the room, to give orders about the journey to Wakkerstroom that he must take upon the morrow. But Mr. Clifford sat there till past midnight, wondering whether he had done right, and if they would find the treasure of which he had dreamed for years, and what the future had in store for them.

If only he could have seen!

When Benita came to breakfast the next morning, she asked where Mr. Meyer was, and learned that he had already departed for Wakkerstroom.

"Certainly he is in earnest," she said with a laugh.

"Yes," answered her father; "Jacob is always in earnest, though, somehow, his earnestness has not brought him much good so far. If we fail, it will not be want of thought and preparation on his part."

Nearly a week went by before Meyer returned again, and meanwhile Benita made ready for her journey. In the intervals of her simple preparations also she talked a good deal, with the help of her father, to the three sturdy-looking Makalanga, who were resting thankfully after their long journey. Their conversation was general, since by tacit consent no further mention was made of the treasure or of anything to do with it, but it enabled her to form a fair opinion of them and their people. She gathered that although they spoke a dialect of Zulu, they had none of the bravery of the Zulus, and indeed lived in deadly terror of the Matabele, who are bastard Zulus—such terror, in fact, that she greatly doubted whether the hundred rifles would be of much use to them, should they ever be attacked by that tribe.

They were what their fathers had been before them, agriculturists and workers in metals—not fighting men. Also she set herself to learn what she could of their tongue, which she did not find difficult, for Benita had a natural aptitude for languages, and had never forgotten the Dutch and Zulu she used to prattle as a child, which now came back to her very fast. Indeed, she could already talk fairly in either of those languages, especially as she spent her spare hours in studying their grammar, and reading them.

So the days went on, till one evening Jacob Meyer appeared with two Scotch carts laden with ten long boxes that looked like coffins, and other smaller boxes which were very heavy, to say nothing of a multitude of stores. As Mr. Clifford prophesied, he had forgotten nothing, for he even brought Benita various articles of clothing, and a revolver for which she had not asked.

Three days later they trekked away from Rooi Krantz upon a peculiarly beautiful Sunday morning in the early spring, giving it out that they were going upon a trading and shooting expedition in the north of the Transvaal. Benita looked back at the pretty little stead and the wooded kloof behind it over which she had nearly fallen, and the placid lake in front of it where the nesting wildfowl wheeled, and sighed. For to her, now that she was leaving it, the place seemed like home, and it came into her mind that she would never see it any more.

VIII.
BAMBATSE

Nearly four months had gone by when at length the waggon with which were Mr. Clifford, Benita, and Jacob Meyer camped one night within the country of the Molimo of Bambatse, whose name was Mambo. Or perhaps that was his title, since (according to Tamas his son) every chief in succession was called Mambo, though not all of them were Molimos, or representatives and prophets of God, or the Great Spirit whom they knew as Munwali. Thus sometimes the Molimo, or priest of Munwali, and the Mambo or chief were different persons. For instance, he said that he, Tamas, would be Mambo on his father's death, but no visions were given to him; therefore as yet, at any rate, he was not called to be Molimo.

In the course of this long journey they had met with many adventures, such as were common to African travellers before the days of railroads; adventures with wild beasts and native tribes, adventures with swollen rivers also, and one that was worst, with thirst, since for three days (owing to the failure of a pit or pan, where they expected to find water) they were obliged to go without drink. Still, none of these were very serious, nor had any of the three of them ever been in better health than they were at this moment, for by good luck they had escaped all fever. Indeed, their rough, wild life had agreed with Benita extraordinarily well, so well that any who had known her in the streets of London would scarcely have recognized her as the sunburnt, active and well-formed young woman who sat that night by the camp fire.

All the horses they had brought with them had been sold, except some which had died, and three that were "salted," or proof against the deadly horse sickness, which they took on with them. Their own servants also had been sent back to Rooi Krantz in charge of a Scotch cart laden with ivory, purchased from Boer hunters who had brought it down from the north of the Transvaal. Therefore, for this was part of the bargain, the three Makalanga were now their only attendants who drove and herded the cattle, while Benita cooked the food which the two white men shot, or sometimes bought from natives.

For days they had been passing through a country that was practically deserted, and now, having crossed a high nek, the same on which Robert Seymour had left his waggon, they were camped in low land which, as they could see by the remains of walls that appeared everywhere, had once been extensively enclosed and cultivated. To their right was a rising mountainous ground, beyond which, said the Makalanga, ran the Zambesi, and in front of them, not more than ten miles away, a great isolated hill, none other than that place that they had journeyed so far to reach, Bambatse, round which flowed the great river. Indeed, thither one of the three Makalanga, he who was named Hoba, had gone on to announce their approach.

They had outspanned amongst ruins, most of them circular in shape, and Benita, studying them in the bright moonlight, guessed that once these had been houses. That place now so solitary, hundreds or thousands of years ago was undoubtedly the home of a great population. Thousands, rather than hundreds, she thought, since close at hand in the middle of one of these round houses, grew a mighty baobab tree, that could not have seen less than ten or fifteen centuries since the seed whence it sprang pierced the cement floor which was still visible about its giant bole.

Tamas, the Molimo's son, saw her studying these evidences of antiquity, and, approaching, saluted her.

"Lady," he said in his own language, which by now she spoke very well, "lady"—and he waved his hand with a fine gesture—"behold the city of my people."

"How do you know that it was their city?" she asked.

"I do not know, lady. Stones cannot speak, the spirits are silent, and we have forgotten. Still, I think so, and our fathers have told us that but six or eight generations ago many folk lived here, though it was not they who built these walls. Even fifty years ago there were many, but now the Matabele have killed them, and we are few; to-morrow you will see how few. Come here and look," and he led her through the entrance of a square cattle kraal which stood close by.

Within were tufts of rank grass, and a few bushes, and among these scores of skulls and other bones.

"The Matabele killed these in the time of Moselikatse," he said. "Now do you wonder that we who remain fear the Matabele, and desire guns to defend ourselves from them, even if we must sell our secrets, in order to buy those guns, who have no money to pay for them?"

"No," she answered, looking at the tall, dignified man, into whose soul the irons of fear and slavery had burnt so deep. "No, I do not wonder."

Next morning at daybreak they trekked on, always through these evidences of dead, forgotten people. They had not more than ten miles to cover to reach their long journey's end, but the road, if so it could be called, ran up-hill, and the oxen, whereof only fourteen were now left to drag the heavy-laden waggon, were thin and footsore, so that their progress was very slow. Indeed, it was past midday when at length they began to enter what by apology might be called the town of Bambatse.

"When we go away from this, it will have to be by water, I think, unless we can buy trek-cattle," said Meyer, looking at the labouring oxen with a doubtful eye.

"Why?" asked Mr. Clifford anxiously.

"Because several of those beasts have been bitten by tsetsefly, like my horse, and the poison is beginning to work. I thought so last night, but now I am sure. Look at their eyes. It was down in that bit of bush veld eight days ago. I said that we ought not to camp there."

At this moment they came to the crest of the ridge, and on its further side saw the wonderful ruins of Bambatse close at hand. In front of them stood a hill jutting out, as it were into the broad waters of the Zambesi river, which, to a great extent, protected it upon three sides. The fourth, that opposite to them, except at one place where a kind of natural causeway led into the town, was also defended by Nature, since here for more than fifty feet in height the granite rock of the base of the hill rose sheer and unclimbable. On the mount itself, that in all may have covered eight or ten acres of ground, and surrounded by a deep donga or ditch, were three rings of fortifications, set one above the other, mighty walls which, it was evident, had been built by no modern hand. Looking at them Benita could well understand how it came about that the poor fugitive Portuguese had chosen this as their last place of refuge, and were overcome at length, not by the thousands of savages who followed and surrounded them, but by hunger. Indeed, the place seemed impregnable to any force that was not armed with siege guns.

On the hither side of this natural fosse, which, doubtless, in ancient times had been filled with water led from the Zambesi, stood the village of the Bambatse Makalanga, a collection of seventy or eighty wretched huts, round, like those of their forefathers, but built of mud and thatch. About them lay the gardens, or square fields, that were well cultivated, and at this season rich with ripening corn. Benita, however, could see no cattle, and concluded, therefore, that these must be kept on the hill for safety, and within its walls.

Down the rough road they lumbered, and through the village, where the few women and children stared at them in a frightened way. Then they came to the causeway, which, on its further side, was blocked with thorns and rough stones taken from the ruins. While they waited for these to be removed by some men who now appeared, Benita looked at the massive, circular wall still thirty or forty feet in height, by perhaps twenty through its base, built of granite blocks without mortar, and ornamented with quaint patterns of other coloured stones. In its thickness she could see grooves, where evidently had once been portcullises, but these had disappeared long ago.

"It is a wonderful place," she said to her father. "I am glad that I came. Have you been all over it?"

"No; only between the first and second walls, and once between the second and third. The old temple, or whatever it is, is on the top, and into that they would never admit us. It is there that the treasure lies."

"That the treasure is supposed to lie," she answered with a smile. "But, Father, what guarantee have you that they will do so now? Perhaps they will take the guns and show us the door—or rather the gate."

"Your daughter is right, there is none; and before a box is taken off the waggon we must get one," said Meyer. "Oh! I know it is risky, and it would have been better to make sure first, but it is too late to talk of that now. Look, the stones are cleared. Trek on—trek!"

The long waggon-whip cracked, the poor, tired-out oxen strained at the yokes, and on they went through the entrance of that fateful fortress that was but just wide enough to admit them. Inside lay a great open space, which, as they could see from the numerous ruins, had once been filled with buildings that now were half hidden by grass, trees, and creepers. This was the outer ring of the temple where, in ancient days, the priests and captains had their home. Travelling across it for perhaps a hundred and fifty yards, they came near the second wall, which was like the first, only not quite so solid, and saw that on a stretch of beaten ground, and seated in the shadow, for the day was hot, the people of Bambatse were gathered to greet them.

When within fifty yards they dismounted from the horses, which were left with the waggon in the charge of the Makalanga, Tamala. Then Benita taking her position between her father and Jacob Meyer, they advanced towards the ring of natives, of whom there may have been two hundred—all of them adult men.

As they came, except one figure who remained seated with his back against the wall, the human circle stood up as a token of respect, and Benita saw that they were of the same stamp as the messengers—tall and good-looking, with melancholy eyes and a cowed expression, wearing the appearance of people who from day to day live in dread of slavery and death. Opposite to them was a break in the circle, through which Tamas led them, and as they crossed it Benita felt that all those people were staring at her with their sad eyes. A few paces from where the man crouched against the wall, his head hidden by a beautifully worked blanket that was thrown over it, were placed three well-carved stools. Upon these, at a motion from Tamas, they sat themselves down, and, as it was not dignified for them to speak first, remained silent.

"Be patient and forgive," said Tamas at length. "My father, Mambo, prays to the Munwali and the spirits of his fathers that this coming of yours may be fortunate, and that a vision of those things that are to be may descend upon him."

Benita, feeling nearly two hundred pairs of eyes concentrated upon her, wished that the vision might come quickly, but after a minute or two fell into tune with the thing, and almost enjoyed this strange experience. Those mighty ancient walls built by hands unknown, which had seen so much history and so much death; the silent, triple ring of patient, solemn men, the last descendants of a cultured race, the crouching figure hidden beneath the blanket, who imagined himself to be communicating with his god—it was all very strange, very well worth the seeing to one who had wearied of the monotony of civilization.

Look, the man stirred, and threw back his blanket, revealing a head white with age, a spiritual, ascetic face, so thin that every bone showed in it, and dark eyes which stared upwards unseeingly, like those of a person in a trance. Thrice he sighed, while his tribesmen watched him. Then he let his eyes fall upon the three white people seated in front of him. First he looked at Mr. Clifford, and his face grew troubled; then at Jacob Meyer, and it was anxious and alarmed. Lastly, he stared at Benita, and while he did so the dark eyes became calm and happy.

"White maiden," he said in a soft, low voice, "for you, at least, I have good tidings. Though Death come near to you, though you see him on your right hand and your left, and in front of you and behind you, I say, fear not. Here you, who have known deep sorrow, shall find happiness and rest, O maiden, with whom goes the spirit of one pure and fair as you, who died so long ago."

Then, while Benita wondered at his words, spoken with such sweet earnestness that although she believed nothing of them, they brought a kind of comfort to her, he looked once more at her father and Jacob Meyer, and, as it were with an effort, was silent.

"Have you no pleasant prophecy for me, old friend," said Jacob, "who have come so far to hear it?"

At once the aged face grew inscrutable, all expression vanished behind a hundred wrinkles, and he answered:

"None, white man—none that I am charged to deliver. Search the skies for yourself, you who are so wise, and read them if you can. Lords," he went on in another voice, "I greet you in the name and presence of my children. Son Tamas, I greet you also; you have done your mission well. Listen, now—you are weary and would rest and eat; still, bear with me, for I have a word to say. Look around you. You see all my tribe, not twenty times ten above the age of boys, we who once were countless as the leaves on yonder trees in spring. Why are we dead? Because of the Amandabele, those fierce dogs whom, two generations ago, Moselikatse, the general of Chaka, brought up to the south of us, who ravish us and kill us year by year.

"We are not warlike, we who have outlived war and the lust of slaying. We are men of peace, who desire to cultivate the land, and to follow our arts which have descended to us from our ancestors, and to worship the Heavens above us, whither we depart to join the spirits of our forefathers. But they are fierce and strong and savage, and they come up and murder our children and old people, and take away the young women and the maidens to be slaves, and with them all our cattle. Where are our cattle? Lobengula, chief of the Amandabele, has them; scarce a cow is left to give milk to the sick or to the motherless babe. And yet he sends for cattle. Tribute, say his messengers, deliver tribute, or my impi will come and take it with your lives. But we have no cattle—all are gone. We have nothing left to us but this ancient mountain and the works built thereon, and a little corn on which we live. Yes, I say it—I, the Molimo—I whose ancestors were great kings—I who have still more wisdom in me than all the hosts of the Amandabele," and as he spoke the old man's grey head sank upon his breast and the tears ran down his withered cheeks, while his people answered:

"Mambo, it is true."

"Now listen again," he went on. "Lobengula threatens us, therefore I sent to these white men who were here before, saying that if they would bring me a hundred guns, and powder and ball, to enable us to beat off the Amandabele from behind these strong walls of ours, I would take them into the secret holy place where for six generations no white man has set a foot, and there suffer them to search for the treasure which is hid therein, no man knows where, that treasure which they asked leave to find four winters gone. We refused it then and drove them hence, because of the curse laid upon us by the white maid who died, the last of the Portuguese, who foretold her people's fate for us if we gave up the buried gold save to one appointed. My children, the Spirit of Bambatse has visited me; I have seen her and others have seen her, and in my sleep she said to me: 'Suffer the men to come and search, for with them is one of the blood to whom my people's wealth is given; and great is your danger, for many spears draw nigh.' My children, I sent my son and other messengers on a far journey to where I knew the men dwelt, and they have returned after many months bringing those men with them, bringing with them also another of whom I knew nothing—yes, her who is appointed, her of whom the Spirit spoke."

Then he lifted his withered hand and held it towards Benita, saying: "I tell you that yonder she sits for whom the generations have waited."

"It is so," answered the Makalanga. "It is the White Lady come again to take her own."

"Friends," asked the Molimo, while they wondered at his strange speech, "tell me, have you brought the guns?"

"Surely," answered Mr. Clifford, "they are there in the waggon, every one of them, the best that can be made, and with them ten thousand cartridges, bought at a great cost. We have fulfilled our share of the bargain; now will you fulfil yours, or shall we go away again with the guns and leave you to meet the Matabele with your assegais?"

"Say you the agreement while we listen," answered the Molimo.

"Good," said Mr. Clifford. "It is this: That you shall find us food and shelter while we are with you. That you shall lead us into the secret place at the head of the hill, where the Portuguese died, and the gold is hidden. That you shall allow us to search for that gold when and where we will. That if we discover the gold, or anything else of value to us, you shall suffer us to take it away, and assist us upon our journey, either by giving us boats and manning them to travel down the Zambesi, or in whatever fashion may be most easy. That you shall permit none to hurt, molest, or annoy us during our sojourn among you. Is that our contract?"

"Not quite all of it," said the Molimo. "There is this to add: first that you shall teach us how to use the guns; secondly, that you shall search for and find the treasure, if so it is appointed, without our help, since in this matter it is not lawful for us to meddle; thirdly, that if the Amandabele should chance to attack us while you are here, you shall do your best to assist us against their power."

"Do you, then, expect attack?" asked Meyer suspiciously.

"White man, we always expect attack. Is it a bargain?"

"Yes," answered Mr. Clifford and Jacob Meyer in one voice, the latter adding: "the guns and the cartridges are yours. Lead us now to the hidden place. We have fulfilled our part; we trust to the honour of you and all your people to fulfil yours."

"White Maiden," asked the Molimo, addressing Benita, "do you also say that it is a bargain?"

"What my father says, I say."

"Good," said the Molimo. "Then, in the presence of my people, and in the name of the Munwali, I, Mambo, who am his prophet, declare that it is so agreed between us, and may the vengeance of the heavens fall upon those who break our pact! Let the oxen of the white men be outspanned, their horses fed, their waggon unloaded, that we may count the guns. Let food be brought into the guest-house also, and after they have eaten, I, who alone of all of you have ever entered it, will lead them to the holy place, that there they may begin to search for that which the white men desire from age to age—to find it if they can; if not, to depart satisfied and at peace."

IX.
THE OATH OF MADUNA

Mr. Clifford and Meyer rose to return to the waggon in order to superintend the unyoking of the oxen and to give directions as to their herding, and the off-saddling of the horses. Benita rose also, wondering when the food that had been promised would be ready, for she was hungry. Meanwhile, the Molimo was greeting his son Tamas, patting his hand affectionately and talking to him, when suddenly Benita, who watched this domestic scene with interest, heard a commotion behind her. Turning to discover its cause, she perceived three great men clad in full war panoply, shields on their left arms, spears in their right hands, black ostrich plumes rising from the polished rings woven in their hair, black moochas about their middles, and black oxtails tied beneath their knees, who marched through the throng of Makalanga as though they saw them not.

"The Matabele! The Matabele are on us!" cried a voice; while other voices shouted, "Fly to your walls!" and yet others, "Kill them! They are few."

But the three men marched on unheeding till they stood before Mambo.

"Who are you, and what do you seek?" the old man asked boldly, though the fear that had taken hold of him at the sight of these strangers was evident enough, for his whole body shook.

"Surely you should know, chief of Bambatse," answered their spokesman with a laugh, "for you have seen the like of us before. We are the children of Lobengula, the Great Elephant, the King, the Black Bull, the Father of the Amandabele, and we have a message for your ear, little Old Man, which, finding that you leave your gate open, we have walked in to deliver."

"Speak your message then, envoys of Lobengula, in my ear and in those of my people," said the Molimo.

"Your people! Are these all your people?" the spokesman replied contemptuously. "Why then, what need was there for the indunas of the King to send so large an impi under a great general against you, when a company of lads armed with sticks would have served the turn? We thought that these were but the sons of your house, the men of your own family, whom you had called together to eat with the white strangers."

"Close the entrance in the wall," cried the Molimo, stung to fury by the insult; and a voice answered:

"Father, it is already done."

But the Matabele, who should have been frightened, only laughed again, and their spokesman said:

"See, my brothers, he thinks to trap us who are but three. Well, kill on, Old Wizard, if you will, but know that if a hand is lifted, this spear of mine goes through your heart, and that the children of Lobengula die hard. Know also that then the impi which waits not far away will destroy you every one, man and woman, youth and maiden, little ones who hold the hand and infants at the breast; none shall be left—none at all, to say, 'Here once lived the cowardly Makalanga of Bambatse.' Nay, be not foolish, but talk softly with us, so that perhaps we may spare your lives."

Then the three men placed themselves back to back, in such fashion that they faced every way, and could not be smitten down from behind, and waited.

"I do not kill envoys," said the Molimo, "but if they are foul-mouthed, I throw them out of my walls. Your message, men of the Amandabele."

"I hear you. Hearken now to the word of Lobengula."

Then the envoy began to speak, using the pronoun I as though it were the Matabele king himself who spoke to his vassal, the Makalanga chief: "I sent to you last year, you slave, who dare to call yourself Mambo of the Makalanga, demanding a tribute of cattle and women, and warning you that if they did not come, I would take them. They did not come, but that time I spared you. Now I send again. Hand over to my messengers fifty cows and fifty oxen, with herds to drive them, and twelve maidens to be approved by them, or

I wipe you out, who have troubled the earth too long, and that before another moon has waned.

"Those are the words of Lobengula," he concluded, and taking the horn snuff-box from the slit in his ear, helped himself, then insolently passed it to the Molimo.

So great was the old chief's rage that, forgetting his self-control, he struck the box from the hand of his tormentor to the ground, where the snuff lay spilled.

"Just so shall the blood of your people be spilled through your rash foolishness," said the messenger calmly, as he picked up the box, and as much of the snuff as he could save.

"Hearken," said the Molimo, in a thin, trembling voice. "Your king demands cattle, knowing that all the cattle are gone, that scarce a cow is left to give drink to a motherless babe. He asks for maidens also, but if he took those he seeks we should have none left for our young men to marry. And why is this so? It is because the vulture, Lobengula, has picked us to the bone; yes, while we are yet alive he has torn the flesh from us. Year by year his soldiers have stolen and killed, till at last nothing is left of us. And now he seeks what we have not got to give, in order that he may force a quarrel upon us and murder us. There is nought left for us to give Lobengula. You have your answer."

"Indeed!" replied the envoy with a sneer. "How comes it, then, that yonder I see a waggon laden with goods, and oxen in the yokes? Yes," he repeated with meaning, "with goods whereof we have known the like at Buluwayo; for Lobengula also sometimes buys guns from white men, O! little Makalanga. Come now, give us the waggon with its load and the oxen and the horses, and though it be but a small gift, we will take it away and ask nothing more this year."

"How can I give you the property of my guests, the white men?" asked the Molimo. "Get you gone, and do your worst, or you shall be thrown from the walls of the fortress."

"Good, but know that very soon we shall return and make an end of you, who are tired of these long and troublesome journeys to gather so little. Go, tend your corn, dwellers in Bambatse, for this I swear in the name of Lobengula, never shall you see it ripen more."

Now the crowd of listening Makalanga trembled at his words, but in the old Molimo they seemed only to rouse a storm of prophetic fury. For a moment he stood staring up at the blue sky, his arms outstretched as though in prayer. Then he spoke in a new voice—a clear, quiet voice, that did not seem to be his own.

"Who am I?" he said. "I am the Molimo of the Bambatse Makalanga; I am the ladder between them and Heaven; I sit on the topmost bough of the tree under which they shelter, and there in the crest of the tree Munwali speaks with me. What to you are winds, to me are voices whispering in my spirit's ears. Once my forefathers were great kings, they were Mambos of all the land, and that is still my name and dignity. We lived in peace; we laboured, we did wrong to no man. Then you Zulu savages came upon us from the southeast and your path was red with blood. Year after year you robbed and you destroyed; you raided our cattle, you murdered our men, you took our maidens and our children to be your women and your slaves, until at length, of all this pit filled with the corn of life, there is left but a little handful. And this you say you will eat up also, lest it should fall into good ground and grow again. I tell you that I think it will not be so; but whether or no that happens, I have words for the ear of your king—a message for a message. Say to him that thus speaks the wise old Molimo of Bambatse.

"I see him hunted like a wounded hyena through the rivers, in the deep bush, and over the mountain. I see him die in pain and misery; but his grave I see not, for no man shall know it. I see the white man take his land and all his wealth; yea, to them and to no son of his shall his people give the Bayéte, the royal salute. Of his greatness and his power, this alone shall remain to him—a name accursed from generation to generation. And last of all I see peace upon the land and upon my children's children." He paused, then added: "For you, cruel dog that you are, this message also from the Munwali, by the lips of his Molimo. I lift no hand against you, but you shall not live to look again upon your king's face. Begone now, and do your worst."

For a moment the three Matabele seemed to be frightened, and Benita heard one of them say to his companions:

"The Wizard has bewitched us! He has bewitched the Great Elephant and all his people! Shall we kill him?"

But quickly shaking off his fears their spokesman laughed, and answered:

"So that is what you have brought the white people here for, old traitor—to plot against the throne of Lobengula."

He wheeled round and stared at Mr. Clifford and Jacob Meyer; then added:

"Good, Grey-beard and Black-Beard: I myself will put you both to such a death as you have never heard of, and as for the girl, since she is well favoured, she shall brew the king's beer, and be numbered amongst the king's wives—unless, indeed, he is pleased to give her to me."

In an instant the thing was done! At the man's words about Benita, Meyer, who had been listening to his threats and bombast unconcerned, suddenly seemed to awake. His dark eyes flashed, his pale face turned cruel. Snatching the revolver from his belt he seemed to point and fire it with one movement, and down—dead or dying—went the Matabele.

Men did not stir, they only stared. Accustomed as they were to death in that wild land, the suddenness of this deed surprised them. The contrast between the splendid, brutal savage who had stood before them a moment ago, and the limp, black thing going to sleep upon the ground, was strange enough to move their imaginations. There he lay, and there, over him, the smoking pistol in his hand, Meyer stood and laughed.

Benita felt that the act was just, and the awful punishment deserved. Yet that laugh of Jacob's jarred upon her, for in it she thought she heard the man's heart speaking; and oh, its voice was merciless! Surely Justice should not laugh when her sword falls!

"Behold, now," said the Molimo in his still voice, pointing at the dead Matabele with his finger; "do I speak lies, or is it true that this man shall not look more upon his king's face? Well, as it was with the servant, so it shall be with the lord, only more slowly. It is the decree of the Munwali, spoken by the voice of his Mouth, the Molimo of Bambatse. Go, children of Lobengula, and bear with you as an offering this first-fruit of the harvest that the white men shall reap among the warriors of his people."

The thin voice died away, and there was silence so intense that Benita thought she heard the scraping of the feet of a green lizard which crept across a stone a yard or two away.

Then of a sudden it ended. Of a sudden the two remaining Matabele turned and fled for their lives, and as, when dogs run, a flock of sheep will wheel about and pursue them, so did the Makalanga. They grabbed at the messengers with their hands, tearing their finery from them; they struck them with sticks, they pounded them with stones, till at length two bruised and bleeding men, finding all escape cut off, and led perhaps by some instinct, staggered back to where Benita stood horrified at this dreadful scene, and throwing themselves upon the ground, clutched at her dress and prayed for mercy.

"Move a little, Miss Clifford," said Meyer. "Three of those brutes will not weigh heavier than one upon my conscience."

"No, no, you shall not," she answered. "Mambo, these men are messengers; spare them."

"Hearken to the voice of pity," said the old prophet, "spoken in a place where pity never was, and not in vain. Let them go. Give mercy to the merciless, for she buys their lives with a prayer."

"They will bring the others on us," muttered Tamas, and even old Mr. Clifford shook his head sadly. But the Molimo only said:

"I have spoken. Let them go. That which will befall must befall, and from this deed no ill shall come that would not have come otherwise."

"You hear? Depart swiftly," said Benita, in Zulu.

With difficulty the two men dragged themselves to their feet, and supporting each other, stood before her. One of them, a clever, powerful-faced man, whose black hair was tinged with grey, addressing himself to Benita, gasped:

"Hear me. That fool there," and he pointed to his dead companion, "whose boasting brought his death upon him, was but a low fellow. I, who kept silence and let him talk, am Maduna, a prince of the royal house who justly deserve to die because I turned my back upon these dogs. Yet I and my brother here take life at your hands, Lady, who, now that I have had time to think, would refuse it at theirs. For, whether I stay or go does not matter. The impi waits; the slayers are beneath the walls. Those things which are decreed will happen; there, yonder old Wizard speaks true. Listen, Lady: should it chance that you have cause to demand two lives at the hands of Maduna, in his own name and the name of his king he promises them to you. In safety shall they pass, they and all that is theirs, without toll taken. Remember the oath of Maduna, Lady, in the hour of your need, and do you, my brother, bear witness to it among our people."

Then, straightening themselves as well as they were able, these two sorely hurt men lifted their right arms and gave Benita the salute due to a chieftainess. This done, taking no note of any other creature there, they limped away to the gate that had been opened for them, and vanished beyond the wall.

All this while Meyer had stood silent; now he spoke with a bitter smile.

"Charity, Miss Clifford, said a certain Paul, as reported in your New Testament, covers a multitude of sins. I hope very much that it will serve to cover our remains from the aasvogels, after we have met our deaths in some such fashion as that brute promised us," and he pointed to the dead man.

Benita looked at her father in question.

"Mr. Meyer means, my dear, that you have done a foolish thing in begging the lives of those Matabele. It would have been safer for us if they were dead, who, as it is, have gone off burning for revenge. Of course, I understand it was natural enough, but— —" and he hesitated and stopped.

"The chief did not say so," broke in Benita with agitation; "besides, if he had, I should not have cared. It was bad enough to see one man killed like that," and she shivered; "I could not bear any more."

"You should not be angry at the fellow's death, seeing that it was what he said of you which brought it upon him," Meyer replied with meaning. "Otherwise he might have gone unharmed as far as I was concerned. For the rest, I did not interfere because I saw it was useless; also I am a fatalist like our friend, the Molimo, and believe in what is decreed. The truth is," he added sharply, "among savages ladies are not in place."

"Why did you not say that down at Rooi Krantz, Jacob?" asked Mr. Clifford. "You know I thought so all the while, but somehow I was over-ruled. Now what I suggest is, that we had better get out of this place as fast as we can—instantly, as soon as we have eaten, before our retreat is cut off."

Meyer looked at the oxen which had been outspanned: nine were wandering about picking up what food they could, but the five which were supposed to have been bitten by tetsefly had lain down.

"Nine worn-out and footsore oxen will not draw the waggon," he said; "also in all probability the place is already surrounded by Matabele, who merely let us in to be sure of the guns which their spies must have told them we were carrying. Lastly, having spent so much and come so far, I do not mean to go without what we seek. Still, if you think that your daughter's danger is greater within these walls than outside of them, you might try, if we can hire servants, which I doubt. Or possibly, if any rowers are to be had, you could go down the Zambesi in a canoe, risking the fever. You and she must settle it, Clifford."

"Difficulties and dangers every way one looks. Benita, what do you say?" asked her father distractedly.

Benita thought a moment. She wished to escape from Mr. Meyer, of whom she was weary and afraid, and would have endured much to do so. On the other hand, her father was tired out, and needed rest; also to turn his back upon this venture now would have been a bitter blow to him. Moreover, lacking cattle and men, how was it to be done? Lastly, something within her, that same voice which had bidden her to come, seemed to bid her to stay. Very soon she had made up her mind.

"Father, dear," she said, "thank you for thinking of me, but as far as I can see, we should run more risks trying to get away than we do in stopping here. I wanted to come, though you warned me against it, and now I must take my chance and trust to God to bring us safe through all dangers. Surely with all those rifles the Makalanga ought to be able to hold such a place as this against the Matabele."

"I hope so," answered her father; "but they are a timid folk. Still, though it would have been far better never to have come, I think with you that it is best to stay where we are, and trust to God."

X.
THE MOUNTAIN TOP

If our adventurers, or any of them, hoped that they were going to be led to the secret places of the fortress that day, they were destined to disappointment. Indeed, the remainder of it was employed arduously enough in unpacking rifles, and a supply of ammunition; also in giving to a few of the leading Makalanga preliminary lessons in the method of their use, a matter as to which their ideas were of the vaguest. The rest of the tribe, having brought their women and children into the outer enclosure of the ancient stronghold, and with them their sheep and goats and the few cattle which remained to them, were employed in building up the entrance permanently with stones, a zigzag secret path upon the river side, that could be stopped in a few minutes, being now their only method of ingress and egress through the thickness of the walls. A certain number of men were also sent out as spies to discover, if possible, the whereabouts of the Matabele impi.

That there was some impi they were almost sure, for a woman who had followed them reported that the injured captain, Maduna, and his companion had been met at a distance of about three miles from Bambatse by a small party of Matabele, who were hiding in some bushes, and that these men had made litters for them, and carried them away; whither she did not know, for she had not dared to pursue them further.

That night Benita passed in the guesthouse, which was only a hut rather larger than the others, while the two men slept in the waggon just outside. She was so tired that for a long while she could not rest. Her mind kept flying back to all the events of the day: the strange words of that mystic old Molimo, concerning herself; the arrival of the brutal messengers and the indaba that followed; then the sudden and awful destruction of their spokesman at the hand of Jacob Meyer. The scene would not leave her eyes, she saw it again and yet again:

the quick transformation of Meyer's indifferent face when the soldier began to insult and threaten her, the lightning-like movement of his hand, the flash, the report, the change from life to death, and the slayer's cruel laugh. He could be very terrible, Jacob Meyer, when his passions were roused!

And what had roused them then? She could not doubt that it was herself—not mere chivalry towards a woman. Even if he were capable of chivalry, merely for that he would never have taken such risk of future trouble and revenge. No; it was something deeper. He had never said anything or done anything, yet long ago instinct or insight had caused Benita to suspect the workings of his mind, and now she was sure of them. The thought was terrible—worse than all her other dangers put together. True, she had her father to rely on, but he had been somewhat ailing of late; age and these arduous journeys and anxieties had told upon him. Supposing that anything were to happen to him—if he died, for instance, how dreadful her position might become, left alone far from the reach of help, with savages— and Jacob Meyer.

Oh! if it had not been for that dreadful shipwreck, how different might be her lot to-day! Well, it was the thought of the shipwreck and of him whom she had lost therein, which had driven her on to this adventure, that in it perhaps her suffering mind might be numbed to rest; and now she must face its issues. God still remained above her, and she would put her trust in Him. After all, if she died, what did it matter?

But that old Molimo had promised her that she was safe from death, that she should find here happiness and rest, though not that of the grave. He promised this, speaking as one who knew of all her grief, and a very little while afterwards, in the case of the Matabele soldier, he had proved himself a prophet of awful power. Also—she knew not how, she knew not why—now, as before, her inmost heart seemed to bear witness that this old dreamer's words were true, and that for her, in some strange manner unforeseen, there still remained a rest.

Comforted a little by this intuition, at length Benita fell asleep.

Next morning, when she came out of the hut, Benita was met by her father, who with a cheerful countenance informed her that at any rate as yet there was no sign of the Matabele. A few hours later, too, some spies came in who said that for miles round nothing could be seen or heard of them. Still the preparations for defence went on, and the hundred best men having been furnished with the rifles, were being drilled in the use of them by Tamas and his two companions, Tamala and Hoba, who had learned how to handle a gun very well in the course of their long journey. The shooting of these raw recruits, however, proved to be execrable; indeed, so dangerous were they that when one of them fired at a mark set upon the wall, it was found necessary to order all the rest to lie down. As it was, a poor trek ox—luckily it was sick—and two sheep were killed.

Foreseeing a scarcity of provisions in the event of a siege, Meyer, provident as ever, had already decreed the death of the tetse-bitten cattle. These were accordingly despatched, and having been skinned and cut up, their flesh was severed into long strips to be dried in the burning sun as biltong, which secretly Benita hoped she might never be called upon to eat. Yet the time was to come when she would swallow that hard, tetse-poisoned flesh with thankfulness.

At midday, after they had eaten, Mr. Clifford and Meyer went to the Molimo, where he sat against the second wall, and, pointing to the men with the guns, said:

"We have fulfilled our bargain. Now fulfil yours. Lead us to the holy place that we may begin our search."

"So be it," he answered. "Follow me, white people."

Then, quite unattended, he guided them round the inner wall till they came to a path of rock not more than a yard wide, beneath which was a precipice fifty feet or so in depth that almost overhung the river. This giddy path they followed for about twenty paces, to find that it ended in a cleft in the wall so narrow that only one person could walk through it at a time. That it must have been the approach to the second stronghold was evident, however, since it was faced on either side with dressed stones, and even the foundation granite had been worn by the human feet which had passed here for ages upon ages. This path zigzagged to and fro in the thickness of the wall till it brought them finally within its circle, a broad belt of steeply-rising ground, covered like that below with the tumbled ruins of buildings amidst which grew bush and trees.

"Heaven send that the gold is not buried here," said Mr. Clifford, surveying the scene; "for if it is, we shall never find it."

The Molimo seemed to guess the meaning of his words from his face, for he answered:

"I think not here. The besiegers won this place and camped in it for many weeks. I could show you where they built their fires and tried to undermine the last wall within which the Portuguese sat about until hunger killed them, for they could not eat their gold. Follow me again."

So on they went up the slope till they came to the base of the third wall, and as before, passed round it, and reached a point above the river. But now there was no passage, only some shallow and almost precipitous steps cut from single stones leading from the foot of the wall to its summit, more than thirty feet above.

"Really," said Benita, contemplating this perilous ascent with dismay, "the ways of treasure seekers are hard. I don't think I can," while her father also looked at them and shook his head.

"We must get a rope," said Meyer to the Molimo angrily. "How can we climb that place without one, with such a gulf below?"

"I am old, but I climb it," said the aged man in mild surprise, since to him, who had trodden it all his life, it seemed not difficult. "Still," he added, "I have a rope above which I use upon dark nights. I will ascend and let it down."

Ascend he did accordingly; indeed, it was a wondrous sight to see his withered legs scrambling from step to step as unconcernedly as though he were going upstairs. No monkey could have been more agile, or more absolutely impervious to the effects of height. Soon he vanished in—or, rather, through—the crest of the wall, and presently appeared again on the top step, whence he let down a stout hide rope, remarking that it was securely tied. So anxious was Meyer to enter the hidden place of which he had dreamed so long that he scarcely waited for it to reach his hand before he began the climb, which he accomplished safely. Then, sitting on the top of the wall, he directed Mr. Clifford to fasten the end of the rope round Benita's waist, and her turn came.

It was not so bad as she expected, for she was agile, and the knowledge that the rope would prevent disaster gave her confidence.

In a very little while she had grasped Meyer's outstretched hand, and been drawn into safety through a kind of aperture above the top step. Then the rope was let down again for her father, who tied it about his middle. Well was it that he did so, since when he was about half-way up, awkwardness, or perhaps loss of nerve—neither of them wonderful in an old man—caused his foot to slip, and had it not been for the rope which Meyer and the Molimo held, he would certainly have fallen into the river some hundreds of feet below. As it was, he recovered himself, and presently arrived panting and very pale. In her relief Benita kissed him, and even as she did so thought again that she had been very near to being left alone with Jacob Meyer.

"All's well that ends well, my dear," he said. "But upon my word I am beginning to wish that I had been content with the humble profits of horse-breeding."

Benita made no answer; it seemed too late for any useful consideration of the point.

"Clever men, those ancients," said Meyer. "See," and he pointed out to her how, by drawing a heavy stone which still lay close by over the aperture through which they had crept, the ascent of the wall could be made absolutely impossible to any enemy, since at its crest it was battened outwards, not inwards, as is usual in these ancient ruins.

"Yes," she answered, "we ought to feel safe enough inside here, and that's as well since I do not feel inclined to go out again at present."

Then they paused to look about them, and this was what they saw:

The wall, built like those below, of unmortared blocks of stone, remained in a wonderfully good state of preservation, for its only enemies had been time, the tropical rains, and the growth of shrubs and trees which here and there had cracked and displaced the stones. It enclosed all the top of the hill, perhaps three acres of ground, and on it at intervals were planted soap-stone pillars, each of them about twelve feet in height, and fashioned at the top to a rude resemblance of a vulture. Many of these columns, however had been blown down, or perhaps struck by lightning, and lay broken upon the wall, or if they had fallen inward, at its foot; but some, six or eight perhaps, were still standing.

Benita learned afterwards that they must have been placed there by the ancient Phoenicians, or whatever people constructed this gigantic fortification, and had something to do with the exact recordings of the different seasons of the year, and their sub-divisions, by means of the shadows which they cast. As yet, however, she did not pay much attention to them, for she was engaged in considering a more remarkable relic of antiquity which stood upon the very verge of the precipice, the wall, indeed, being built up to its base on either side.

It was the great cone of which Richard Seymour had told her, fifty feet high or more, such as once was found in the Phoenician temples. But in this case it was not built of masonry, but shaped by the hand of man out of a single gigantic granite monolith of the sort that are sometimes to be met with in Africa, that thousands or millions of years ago had been left standing thus when the softer rock around it was worn away by time and weather. On the inner side of this cone were easy steps whereby it could be ascended, and its top, which might have been six feet in diameter, was fashioned in the shape of a cup, probably for the purposes of acts of worship and of sacrifice. This extraordinary monument, which, except on the river side, could not be seen from below on account of the slope of the hill, leaned slightly outwards, so that a stone dropped from its crest would fall into the waters of the stream.

"Thence it was," said the Molimo, "that my forefathers saw the last of the Portuguese, the fair daughter of the great Captain Ferreira, hurl herself to death after she had given the gold into our keeping, and laid the curse upon it, until she came again. So in my dreams have I seen and heard her also, ay, and others have seen her, but these only from by the river far below."

He paused awhile, looking at Benita with his queer, dreamy eyes; then said suddenly:

"Say, Lady, do you remember nothing of that matter?"

Now Benita grew vexed, for the whole thing was uncanny and jarred upon her.

"How can I remember," she asked, "who was born not five and twenty years ago?"

"I do not know," he answered. "How should I know, who am but an ignorant old black man, who was born not much more than eighty years ago? Yet, Lady, tell me, for I seek your wisdom, where were you born from? Out of the earth, or out of the heavens? What? You shake your head, you who do not remember? Well, neither do I remember. Yet it is true that all circles meet somewhere, and it is true that the Portuguese maiden said she would come again; and lastly it is true that she was such an one as you are, for she haunts this place, and I, who have seen her sitting yonder in the moonlight, know her beauty well. Yet mayhap she comes no more in flesh, but still her spirit comes; for, Lady, out of those eyes of yours I see it gaze at me. Come," he added abruptly, "let us descend the wall, for as you cannot remember, there is more to show you. Have no fear—the steps are easy."

So they went down without much difficulty, since, from the accumulation of rubbish and other causes, the wall was a great deal lower on this side, and found themselves in the usual dense growth of vegetation and brushwood through which ran a little path. It led them past the ruins of buildings whereof the use and purpose were long since forgotten, for their roofs had fallen in hundreds or thousands of years ago, to the entrance of a cave which was placed almost at the foot of the monolithic cone, but thirty or forty yards further from the circle of the wall. Here the Molimo bade them stay while he lit the lamps within. Five minutes passed and he returned, saying that all was ready.

"Be not afraid of what you may see," he added, "for know, white people, that save my forefathers and myself, none have entered this place since the Portuguese perished here, nor have we, who do but come hither to pray and receive the word of the Munwali, ever ventured to disturb it. As it was, so it is. Come, Lady, come; she whose spirit goes with you was the last of your white race to pass this door. It is therefore fitting that your feet and her spirit should be the first to enter it again."

Benita hung back a little, for the adventure was eerie, then, determined that she would show no fear in the presence of this old priest, took the thin hand he stretched out to her, and walked forward with head erect. The two men began to follow her, but the Molimo stopped them, saying:

"Not so. The maiden enters first alone with me; it is her house, and should it please her to ask you to dwell therein, so be it. But first she must visit her house alone."

"Nonsense," said Mr. Clifford angrily. "I will not have it. It will frighten her."

"Lady, do you trust me?" asked the Molimo.

"Yes," she answered; adding, "Father, I think you had better let me go alone. I am not afraid now, and it may be wisest not to thwart him. This is a very strange business—not like anything else—and really I think that I had better go alone. If I do not come back presently, you can follow."

"Those who break in upon the sleep of the dead should walk gently, gently," piped the old Molimo in a sing-song voice. "The maiden's breath is pure; the maiden's foot is light; her breath will not offend the dead; her step will not disturb the dead. White men, white men, anger not the dead, for the dead are mighty, and will be revenged upon you when you are dead; soon, very soon, when you are dead—dead in your sorrows, dead in your sins, dead, gathered to that company of the dead who await us here."

And, still chanting his mystic song, he led Benita by the hand out of the light, onward into darkness, away from life, onward into the place of death.

XI.
THE SLEEPERS IN THE CAVE

Like every other passage in this old fortress, the approach to the cave was narrow and winding; presumably the ancients had arranged them thus to facilitate their defence. After the third bend, however, Benita saw a light ahead which flowed from a native lamp lit in the arched entrance. At the side of this arch was a shell-shaped hollow, cut in the rock about three feet above the floor. Its appearance seemed familiar to her; why, she was soon to learn, although at the moment she did not connect it with anything in particular. The cave beyond was large, lofty, and not altogether natural, for its walls had evidently been shaped, or at any rate trimmed, by man. Probably here the old Priests had established their oracle, or place of offering.

At first Benita could not see much, since in that great cavern two lamps of hippopotamus oil gave but little light. Presently, however, her eyes became accustomed to the gloom, and as they advanced up its length she perceived that save for a skin rug upon which she guessed the Molimo sat at his solitary devotions, and some gourds and platters for water and food, all the front part of the place appeared to be empty. Beyond, in its centre, stood an object of some gleaming metal, that from its double handles and roller borne upon supports of rock she took to be some kind of winch, and rightly, for beneath it was the mouth of a great well, the water supply of the topmost fortification.

Beyond the well was a stone altar, shaped like a truncated cone or pyramid, and at some distance away against the far wall, as she dimly discovered by the lamp that stood upon the altar, cut in relief upon that wall indeed, a colossal cross to which, vigorously if rudely executed in white stone, hung the image of Christ crucified, the crown of thorns upon His drooping head. Now she understood. Whatever may have been the first worship to which this place was dedicated, Christians had usurped it, and set up here the sacred symbol of their faith, awful enough to look upon in such surroundings. Doubtless, also, the shell-shaped basin at the entrance had served the worshippers in this underground chapel as a stoup for holy water.

The Molimo lifted the lamp from the altar, and having adjusted its wick, held it up in front of the rood before which, although she was no Catholic, Benita bowed her head and crossed herself, while he watched her curiously. Then he lowered it, and she perceived that on the cemented floor lay great numbers of shrouded forms that at first looked to her like folk asleep. He stepped to one of them and touched it with his foot, whereon the cloth with which it was covered crumbled into dust, revealing beneath a white skeleton.

All those sleepers rested well indeed, for they had been dead at least two hundred years. There they lay—men, women, and children, though of the last but few. Some of them had ornaments on their bones, some were clad in armour, and by all the men were swords, or spears, or knives, and here and there what she took to be primitive fire-arms. Certain of them also had turned into mummies in that dry air—grotesque and dreadful objects from which she gladly averted her eyes.

The Molimo led her forward to the foot of the crucifix, where, upon its lowest step and upon the cemented floor immediately beneath it respectively, lay two shapes decorously covered with shawls of some heavy material interwoven with gold wire, for the manufacture of which the Makalanga were famous when first the Portuguese came into contact with them. The Molimo took hold of the cloths that seemed almost as good now as on the day when they were woven, and lifted them, revealing beneath the figures of a man and woman. The features were unrecognizable, although the hair, white in the man's case and raven black in that of the woman, remained perfect. They had been great people, for orders glittered upon the man's breast, and his sword was gold hilted, whilst the woman's bones were adorned with costly necklaces and jewels, and in her hand was still a book bound in sheets of silver. Benita took it up and looked at it. It was a missal beautifully illuminated, which doubtless the poor lady had been reading when at length she sank exhausted into the sleep of death.

"See the Lord Ferreira and his wife," said the Molimo, "whom their daughter laid thus before she went to join them." Then, at a motion from Benita, he covered them up again with their golden cloths.

"Here they sleep," he went on in his chanting voice, "a hundred and fifty and three of them—a hundred and fifty and three; and when I dream in this place at night, I have seen the ghosts of every one of them arise from beside their forms and come gliding down the cave— the husband with the wife, the child with the mother—to look at me, and ask when the maiden returns again to take her heritage and give them burial."

Benita shuddered; the solemn awfulness of the place and scene oppressed her. She began to think that she, too, saw those ghosts.

"It is enough," she said. "Let us be going."

So they went, and the pitiful, agonized Christ upon the cross, at which she glanced from time to time over her shoulder, faded to a white blot, then vanished away in the darkness, through which, from generation to generation, it kept its watch above the dead, those dead that in their despair once had cried to it for mercy, and bedewed its feet with tears.

Glad, oh! glad was she when she had left that haunted place behind her, and saw the wholesome light again.

"What have you seen?" asked her father and Meyer, in one breath, as they noted her white and frightened face.

She sank upon a stone seat at the entrance of the cave, and before she could open her lips the Molimo answered for her:

"The maiden has seen the dead. The Spirit who goes with her has given greeting to its dead that it left so long ago. The maiden has done reverence to the White One who hangs upon the cross, and asked a blessing and a pardon of Him, as she whose Spirit goes with her did reverence before the eyes of my forefathers, and asked a blessing and a pardon ere she cast herself away." And he pointed to the little golden crucifix which hung upon Benita's bosom, attached to the necklace which Tamas, the messenger, had given her at Rooi Krantz.

"Now," he went on, "now the spell is broken, and the sleepers must depart to sleep elsewhere. Enter, white men; enter, if you dare, and ask for pardon and for blessing if it may be found, and gather up the dry bones and take the treasure that was theirs, if it may be found, and conquer the curse that goes with the treasure for all save one, if you can, if you can, if you can! Rest you here, maiden, in the sweet sunshine, and follow me, white men; follow me into the dark of the dead to seek for that which the white men love." And once more he vanished down the passage, turning now and again to beckon to them, while they went after him as though drawn against their wish. For now, at the last moment, some superstitious fear spread from him to them, and showed itself in their eyes.

To Benita, half fainting upon the stone seat, for this experience had shaken her to the heart, it seemed but a few minutes, though really the best part of an hour had gone by, when her father reappeared as white-faced as she had been.

"Where is Mr. Meyer?" she asked.

"Oh!" he answered. "He is collecting all the golden ornaments off those poor bodies, and tumbling their bones together in a corner of the cave."

Benita uttered an exclamation of horror.

"I know what you mean," said her father. "But, curse the fellow! he has no reverence, although at first he seemed almost as scared as I was myself. He said that as we could not begin our search with all those corpses about, they had best be got out of the way as soon as possible. Or perhaps it was because he is really afraid of them, and wanted to prove to himself that they are nothing more than dust. Benita," went on the old man, "to tell you the truth, I wish heartily that we had left this business alone. I don't believe that any good will come of it, and certainly it has brought enough trouble already. That old prophet of a Molimo has the second sight, or something like it, and he does not hide his opinion, but keeps chuckling away in that dreadful place, and piping out his promises of ill to be."

"He promised me nothing but good," said Benita with a little smile. "Though I don't see how it can happen. But if you dislike the thing, father, why not give it up and try to escape?"

"It is too late, dear," he replied passionately. "Meyer would never come, and I can't in honour leave him. Also, I should laugh at myself for the rest of my life; and, after all, why should we not have the gold if it can be found? It belongs to nobody. We do not get it by robbery, or murder; nuggets are of no use to Portuguese who have been dead two hundred years, and whose heirs, if they have any, it is impossible to discover. Nor can it matter to them whether they lie about singly as they died or were placed after death, or piled together in a corner. Our fears were mere churchyard superstitions, which we have caught from that ghoul of a Molimo. Don't you agree with me?"

"Yes, I suppose so," answered Benita, "though a fate may cling to certain things or places, perhaps. At any rate, I think that it is of no use turning back now, even if we had anywhere to turn, so we may as well go through with the venture and await its end. Give me the water-bottle, please. I am thirsty."

A while later Jacob Meyer appeared, carrying a great bundle of precious objects wrapped in one of the gold cere-cloths, which bundle he hid away behind a stone.

"The cave is much tidier now," he said, as he flicked the thick dust which had collected on them during his unhallowed task from his hands, and hair, and garments. Then he drank greedily, and asked:

"Have you two made any plans for our future researches?"

They shook their heads.

"Well, then, I have. I thought them out while I was bone-carting, and here they are. It is no use our going down below again; for one thing, the journey is too dangerous, and takes too long; and for another, we are safer up above, where we have plenty to do."

"But," said Benita, "how about things to eat and sleep on, and the rest?"

"Simple enough, Miss Clifford; we must get them up. The Kaffirs will bring them to the foot of the third wall, and we will haul them to its top with a rope. Of water it seems there is plenty in that well, which is fed by a spring a hundred and fifty feet down, and the old chain is still on the roller, so we only need a couple of buckets from the waggon. Of wood for cooking there is plenty also, growing on the spot; and we can camp in the cave or outside of it, as we like, according to the state of the weather. Now, do you rest here while I go down. I will be back in an hour with some of the gear, and then you must help me."

So he went, and the end of it was that before nightfall they had enough things for their immediate needs, and by the second night, working very hard, were more or less comfortably established in their strange habitation. The canvas flap from the waggon was arranged as a tent for Benita, the men sleeping beneath a thick-leaved tree near by. Close at hand, under another tree, was their cooking place. The provisions of all sorts, including a couple of cases of square-face and a large supply of biltong from the slaughtered cattle, they stored with a quantity of ammunition in the mouth of the cave. Fresh meat also was brought to them daily, and hauled up in baskets—that is, until there was none to bring—and with it grain for bread, and green mealies to serve as vegetables. Therefore, as the water from the well proved to be excellent and quite accessible, they were soon set up in all things necessary, and to these they added from time to time as opportunity offered.

In all these preparations the old Molimo took a part, nor, when they were completed, did he show any inclination to leave them. In the morning he would descend to his people below, but before nightfall he always returned to the cave, where for many years it had been his custom to sleep—at any rate several times a week, in the gruesome company of the dead Portuguese. Jacob Meyer persuaded Mr. Clifford that his object was to spy upon them, and talked of turning him out; but Benita, between whom and the old man had sprung up a curious friendship and sympathy, prevented it, pointing out that they were much safer with the Molimo, as a kind of hostage, than they could be without him; also, that his knowledge of the place, and of other things, might prove of great help to them. So in the end he was allowed to remain, as indeed he had a perfect right to do.

All this while there was no sign of any attack by the Matabele. Indeed, the fear of such a thing was to some extent dying away, and Benita, watching from the top of the wall, could see that their nine remaining oxen, together with the two horses—for that belonging to Jacob Meyer had died—and the Makalanga goats and sheep, were daily driven out to graze; also, that the women were working in the crops upon the fertile soil around the lowest wall. Still, a strict watch was kept, and at night everyone slept within the fortifications; moreover, the drilling of the men and their instruction in the use of firearms went on continually under Tamas, who now, in his father's old age, was the virtual chief of the people.

It was on the fourth morning that at length, all their preparations being completed, the actual search for the treasure began. First, the Molimo was closely interrogated as to its whereabouts, since they thought that even if he did not know this exactly, some traditions of the fact might have descended to him from his ancestors. But he declared with earnestness that he knew nothing, save that the Portuguese maiden had said that it was hidden; nor, he added, had any dream or vision come to him concerning this matter, in which he took no interest. If it was there, it was there; if it was not there, it was not there—it remained for the white men to search and see.

For no very good reason Meyer had concluded that the gold must have been concealed in or about the cave, so here it was that they began their investigations.

First, they bethought them of the well into which it might possibly have been thrown, but the fact of this matter proved very difficult to ascertain. Tying a piece of metal—it was an old Portuguese sword-hilt—to a string, they let it down and found that it touched water at a depth of one hundred and twenty feet, and bottom at a depth of one hundred and forty-seven feet. Therefore there were twenty-seven feet of water. Weighting a bucket they sank it until it rested upon this bottom, then wound it up again several times. On the third occasion it brought up a human bone and a wire anklet of pure gold. But this proved nothing, except that some ancient, perhaps thousands of years ago, had been thrown, or had fallen, into the well.

Still unsatisfied, Jacob Meyer, who was a most intrepid person, determined to investigate the place himself, a task of no little difficulty and danger, since proper ladders were wanting, nor, had they existed, was there anything to stand them on. Therefore it came to this: a seat must be rigged on to the end of the old copper chain, and be lowered into the pit after the fashion of the bucket. But, as Benita pointed out, although they might let him down, it was possible that they would not be able to draw him up again, in which case his plight must prove unfortunate. So, when the seat had been prepared, an experiment was made with a stone weighing approximately as much as a man. This Benita and her father let down easily enough, but, as they anticipated, when it came to winding it up again, their strength was barely sufficient to the task. Three people could do it well, but with two the thing was risky. Now Meyer asked—or, rather, commanded—the Molimo to order some of his men to help him, but this the old chief refused point blank to do.

First, he made a number of excuses. They were all employed in drilling, and in watching for the Matabele; they were afraid to venture here, and so forth. At last Meyer grew furious; his eyes flashed, he ground his teeth, and began to threaten.

"White man," said the Molimo, when he had done, "it cannot be. I have fulfilled my bargain with you. Search for the gold; find it and take it away if you can. But this place is holy. None of my tribe, save he who holds the office of Molimo for the time, may set a foot therein. Kill me if you will—I care not; but so it is, and if you kill me, afterwards they will kill you."

Now Meyer, seeing that nothing was to be gained by violence, changed his tone, and asked if he himself would help them.

"I am old, my strength is small," he replied; "yet I will put my hand to the chain and do my best. But, if I were you, I would not descend that pit."

"Still, I will descend it, and to-morrow," said Meyer.

XII.
THE BEGINNING OF THE SEARCH

Accordingly, on the next day the great experiment was made. The chain and ancient winding gear had been tested and proved to be amply sufficient to the strain. Therefore, nothing remained save for Meyer to place himself in the wooden seat with an oil-lamp, and in case this should be extinguished, matches and candles, of both of which they had a large supply.

He did so boldly enough, and swung out over the mouth of the pit, while the three of them clutched the handles of the winch. Then they began to lower, and slowly his white face disappeared into the black depth. At every few turns his descent was stopped that he might examine the walls of the well, and when he was about fifty feet down he called to them to hold on, which they did, listening while he struck at the rock with a hammer, for here it sounded very hollow.

At length he shouted to them to lower away again, and they obeyed, until nearly all the chain was out, and they knew he must be near the water. Now Benita, peeping over the edge, saw that the star of light had vanished. His lamp was out, nor did he appear to attempt to re-light it. They shouted down the well to him, but no answer coming, began to wind up as fast as they were able. It was all that their united strength could manage, and very exhausted were they when at length Jacob reappeared at the top. At first, from the look of him they thought that he was dead, and had he not tied himself to the chain, dead he certainly would have been, for evidently his senses had left him long ago. Indeed, he had fallen almost out of the seat, over which his legs hung limply, his weight being supported by the hide rope beneath his arms which was made fast to the chain.

They swung him in and dashed water over his face, till, to their relief, at last he began to gasp for breath, and revived sufficiently to enable them to half-lead and half-carry him out into the fresh air.

"What happened to you?" asked Clifford.

"Poisoned with gases, I suppose," Meyer answered with a groan, for his head was aching sadly. "The air is often bad at the bottom of deep wells, but I could smell or feel nothing until suddenly my senses left me. It was a near thing—a very near thing."

Afterwards, when he had recovered a little, he told them that at one spot deep down in the well, on the river side of it, he found a place where it looked as though the rock had been cut away for a space of about six feet by four, and afterwards built up again with another sort of stone set in hard mortar or cement. Immediately beneath, too, were socket-holes in which the ends of beams still remained, suggesting that here had been a floor or platform. It was while he was examining these rotted beams that insensibility overcame him. He added that he thought that this might be the entrance to the place where the gold was hidden.

"If so," said Mr. Clifford, "hidden it must remain, since it can have no better guardian than bad air. Also, floors like that are common in all wells to prevent rubbish from falling into the water, and the stonework you saw probably was only put there by the ancients to mend a fault in the rock and prevent the wall from caving in."

"I hope so," said Meyer, "since unless that atmosphere purifies a good deal I don't think that even I dare go down again, and until one gets there, of that it is difficult to be sure, though of course a lantern on a string will tell one something."

This was the end of their first attempt. The search was not renewed until the following afternoon, when Meyer had recovered a little from the effects of the poisoning and the chafing of the hide ropes beneath his arms. Indeed, from the former he never did quite recover, since thenceforward Benita, who for her own reasons watched the man closely, discovered a marked and progressive change in his demeanour. Hitherto he had appeared to be a reserved man, one who kept tight hand upon himself, and, if she knew certain things about him, it was rather because she guessed, or deduced them, than because he allowed them to be seen. On two occasions only had he shown his heart before her—when they had spoken together by the shores of Lake Chrissie on the day of the arrival of the messengers, and he declared his ardent desire for wealth and power; and quite recently, when he killed the Matabele envoy. Yet she felt certain that this heart of his was very passionate and insurgent; that his calm was like the ice that hides the stream, beneath which its currents run fiercely, none can see whither. The fashion in which his dark eyes would flash, even when his pale countenance remained unmoved, told her so, as did other things.

For instance, when he was recovering from his swoon, the first words that passed his lips were in German, of which she understood a little, and she thought that they shaped themselves to her name, coupled with endearing epithets. From that time forward he became less guarded—or, rather, it seemed as though he were gradually losing power to control himself. He would grow excited without apparent cause, and begin to declaim as to what he would do when he had found the gold; how he would pay the world back all it had caused him to suffer—how he would become a "king."

"I am afraid that you will find that exalted position rather lonely," said Benita with a careless laugh, and next minute was sorry that she had spoken, for he answered, looking at her in a way that she did not like:

"Oh, no! There will be a queen—a beautiful queen, whom I shall endow with wealth, and deck with jewels, and surround with love and worship."

"What a fortunate lady!" she said, still laughing, but taking the opportunity to go away upon some errand.

At other times, especially after dark, he would walk up and down in front of the cave, muttering to himself, or singing wild old German songs in his rich voice. Also, he made a habit of ascending the granite pillar and seating himself there, and more than once called down to her to come up and share his "throne." Still, these outbreaks were so occasional that her father, whose perceptions appeared to Benita to be less keen than formerly, scarcely noticed them, and for the rest his demeanour was what it had always been.

Further researches into the well being out of the question, their next step was to make a thorough inspection of the chapel-cave itself. They examined the walls inch by inch, tapping them with a hammer to hear if they sounded hollow, but without result. They examined the altar, but it proved to be a solid mass of rock. By the help of a little ladder they had made, they examined the crucifix, and discovered that the white figure on the cross had evidently been fashioned out of some heathen statue of soft limestone, for at its back were the remains of draperies, and long hair which the artist had not thought it necessary to cut away. Also, they found that the arms had been added, and were of a slightly different stone, and that the weight of the figure was taken partly by an iron staple which supported the body, and partly by strong copper wire twisted to resemble cord, and painted white, which was passed round the wrists and supported the arms. This wire ran through loops of rock cut in the traverse of the cross, that itself was only raised in relief by chiselling away the solid stone behind.

Curiously enough, this part of the search was left to Mr. Clifford and Benita, since it was one that Jacob Meyer seemed reluctant to undertake. A Jew by birth, and a man who openly professed his want of belief in that or any other religion, he yet seemed to fear this symbol of the Christian faith, speaking of it as horrible and unlucky; yes, he who, without qualm or remorse, had robbed and desecrated the dead that lay about its feet. Well, the crucifix told them nothing; but as Mr. Clifford, lantern in hand, descended the ladder, which Benita held, Jacob Meyer, who was in front of the altar, called to them excitedly that he had found something.

"Then it is more than we have," said Mr. Clifford, as he laid down the ladder and hurried to him.

Meyer was sounding the floor with a staff of wood—an operation which he had only just begun after the walls proved barren.

"Listen now," he said, letting the heavy staff drop a few paces to the right of the altar, where it produced the hard, metallic clang that comes from solid stone when struck. Then he moved to the front of the altar and dropped it again, but now the note was hollow and reverberant. Again and again he repeated the experiment, till they had exactly mapped out where the solid rock ended and that which seemed to be hollow began—a space of about eight feet square.

"We've got it," he said triumphantly. "That's the entrance to the place where the gold is," and the others were inclined to agree with him.

Now it remained to put their theory to the proof—a task of no small difficulty. Indeed, it took them three days of hard, continual work. It will be remembered that the floor of the cave was cemented over, and first of all this cement, which proved to be of excellent quality, being largely composed of powdered granite, must be broken up. By the help of a steel crowbar, which they had brought with them in the waggon, at length that part of their task was completed, revealing the rock beneath. By this time Benita was confident that, whatever might lie below, it was not the treasure, since it was evident that the poor, dying Portuguese would not have had the time or the strength to cement it over. When she told the others so, however, Meyer, convinced that he was on the right tack, answered that doubtless it was done by the Makalanga after the Portuguese days, as it was well known that they retained a knowledge of the building arts of their forefathers until quite a recent period, when the Matabele began to kill them out.

When at length the cement was cleared away and the area swept, they discovered—for there ran the line of it—that here a great stone was set into the floor; it must have weighed several tons. As it was set in cement, however, to lift it, even if they had the strength to work the necessary levers, proved quite impossible. There remained only one thing to be done—to cut a way through. When they had worked at this task for several hours, and only succeeded in making a hole six inches deep, Mr. Clifford, whose old bones ached and whose hands were very sore, suggested that perhaps they might break it up with gunpowder. Accordingly, a pound flask of that explosive was poured into the hole, which they closed over with wet clay and a heavy rock, leaving a quill through which ran an extemporized fuse of cotton wick. All being prepared, their fuse was lit, and they left the cave and waited.

Five minutes afterwards the dull sound of an explosion reached their ears, but more than an hour went by before the smoke and fumes would allow them to enter the place, and then it was to find that the results did not equal their expectations. To begin with, the slab was only cracked—not shattered, since the strength of the powder had been expended upwards, not downwards, as would have happened in the case of dynamite, of which they had none. Moreover, either the heavy stone which they had placed upon it, striking the roof of the cave, or the concussion of the air, had brought down many tons of rock, and caused wide and dangerous-looking cracks. Also, though she said nothing of it, it seemed to Benita that the great white statue on the cross was leaning a little further forward than it used to do. So the net result of the experiment was that they were obliged to drag away great fragments of the fallen roof that lay upon the stone, which remained almost as solid and obdurate as before.

So there was nothing for it but to go on working with the crowbar. At length, towards the evening of the third day of their labour, when the two men were utterly tired out, a hole was broken through, demonstrating the fact that beneath this cover lay a hollow of some sort. Mr. Clifford, to say nothing of Benita, who was heartily weary of the business, wished to postpone proceedings till the morrow, but Jacob Meyer would not. So they toiled on until about eleven o'clock at night, when at length the aperture was of sufficient size to admit a man. Now, as in the case of the well, they let down a stone tied to a string, to find that the place beneath was not more than eight feet deep. Then, to ascertain the condition of the air, a candle was lowered, which at first went out, but presently burnt well enough. This point settled, they brought their ladder, whereby Jacob descended with a lantern.

In another minute they heard the sound of guttural German oaths rising through the hole. Mr. Clifford asked what was the matter, and received the reply that the place was a tomb, with nothing in it but an accursed dead monk, information at which Benita could not help bursting into laughter.

The end of it was that both she and her father went down also, and there, sure enough, lay the remains of the old missionary in his cowl, with an ivory crucifix about his neck, and on his breast a scroll stating that he, Marco, born at Lisbon in 1438, had died at Bambatse in the year 1503, having laboured in the Empire of Monomotapa for seventeen years, and suffered great hardships and brought many souls to Christ. The scroll added that it was he, who before he entered into religion was a sculptor by trade, that had fashioned the figure on the cross in this chapel out of that of the heathen goddess which had stood in the same place from unknown antiquity. It ended with a request, addressed to all good Christians in Latin, that they who soon must be as he was would pray for his soul and not disturb his bones, which rested here in the hope of a blessed resurrection.

When this pious wish was translated to Jacob Meyer by Mr. Clifford, who still retained some recollection of the classics which he had painfully acquired at Eton and Oxford, the Jew could scarcely contain his wrath. Indeed, looking at his bleeding hands, instead of praying for the soul of that excellent missionary, to reach whose remains he had laboured with such arduous, incessant toil, he cursed it wherever it might be, and unceremoniously swept the bones, which the document asked him not to disturb, into a corner of the tomb, in order to ascertain whether there was not, perhaps, some stair beneath them.

"Really, Mr. Meyer," said Benita, who, in spite of the solemnity of the surroundings, could not control her sense of humour, "if you are not careful the ghosts of all these people will haunt you."

"Let them haunt me if they can," he answered furiously. "I don't believe in ghosts, and defy them all."

At this moment, looking up, Benita saw a figure gliding out of the darkness into the ring of light, so silently that she started, for it might well have been one of those ghosts in whom Jacob Meyer did not believe. In fact, however, it was the old Molimo, who had a habit of coming upon them thus.

"What says the white man?" he asked of Benita, while his dreamy eyes wandered over the three of them, and the hole in the violated tomb.

"He says that he does not believe in spirits, and that he defies them," she answered.

"The white gold-seeker does not believe in spirits, and he defies them," Mambo repeated in his sing-song voice. "He does not believe in the spirits that I see all around me now, the angry spirits of the dead, who speak together of where he shall lie and of what shall happen to him when he is dead, and of how they will welcome one who disturbs their rest and defies and curses them in his search for the riches which he loves. There is one standing by him now, dressed in a brown robe with a dead man cut in ivory like to that," and he pointed to the crucifix in Jacob's hands, "and he holds the ivory man above him and threatens him with sleepless centuries of sorrow, when he is also one of those spirits in which he does not believe."

Then Meyer's rage blazed out. He turned upon the Molimo and reviled him in his own tongue, saying that he knew well where the treasure was hidden, and that if he did not point it out he would kill him and send him to his friends, the spirits. So savage and evil did he look that Benita retreated a little way, while Mr. Clifford strove in vain to calm him. But although Meyer laid his hand upon the knife in his belt and advanced upon him, the old Molimo neither budged an inch nor showed the slightest fear.

"Let him rave on," he said, when at length Meyer paused exhausted. "Just so in a time of storm the lightnings flash and the thunder peals, and the water foams down the face of rock; but then comes the sun again, and the hill is as it has ever been, only the storm is spent and lost. I am the rock, he is but the wind, the fire, and the rain. It is not permitted that he should hurt me, and those spirits in whom he does not believe treasure up his curses, to let them fall again like stones upon his head."

Then, with a contemptuous glance at Jacob, the old man turned and glided back into the darkness out of which he had appeared.

XIII.
BENITA PLANS ESCAPE

The next morning, while she was cooking breakfast, Benita saw Jacob Meyer seated upon a rock at a little distance, sullen and disconsolate. His chin was resting on his hand, and he watched her intently, never taking his eyes from her face. She felt that he was concentrating his will upon her; that some new idea concerning her had come into his mind; for it was one of her miseries that she possessed the power of interpreting the drift of this man's thoughts. Much as she detested him, there existed that curious link between them.

It may be remembered that, on the night when they first met at the crest of Leopard's Kloof, Jacob had called her a "thought-sender," and some knowledge of their mental intimacy had come home to Benita. From that day forward her chief desire had been to shut a door between their natures, to isolate herself from him and him from her. Yet the attempt was never entirely successful.

Fear and disgust took hold of her, bending there above the fire, all the while aware of the Jew's dark eyes that searched her through and through. Benita formed a sudden determination. She would implore her father to come away with her.

Of course, such an attempt would be terribly dangerous. Of the Matabele nothing had been seen; but they might be about, and even if enough cattle could be collected to draw the waggon, it belonged to Meyer as much as to her father, and must therefore be left for him. Still, there remained the two horses, which the Molimo had told her were well and getting fat.

At this moment Meyer rose and began to speak to her.

"What are you thinking of, Miss Clifford?" he asked in his soft foreign voice.

She started, but answered readily enough:

"Of the wood which is green, and the kid cutlets which are getting smoked. Are you not tired of kid, Mr. Meyer?" she went on.

He waved the question aside. "You are so good—oh! I mean it—so really good that you should not tell stories even about small things. The wood is not green; I cut it myself from a dead tree; and the meat is not smoked; nor were you thinking of either. You were thinking of me, as I was thinking of you; but what exactly was in your mind, this time I do not know, and that is why I ask you to tell me."

"Really, Mr. Meyer," she answered flushing; "my mind is my own property."

"Ah! do you say so? Now I hold otherwise—that it is my property, as mine is yours, a gift that Nature has given to each of us."

"I seek no such gift," she answered; but even then, much as she would have wished to do so, she could not utter a falsehood, and deny this horrible and secret intimacy.

"I am sorry for that, as I think it very precious; more precious even than the gold which we cannot find; for Miss Clifford, it brings me nearer you."

She turned upon him, but he held up his hand, and went on:

"Oh! do not be angry with me, and do not fear that I am going to trouble you with soft speeches, for I shall not, unless a time should come, as I think that perhaps it will, when you may wish to listen to them. But I want to point out something to you, Miss Clifford. Is it not a wonderful thing that our minds should be so in tune, and is there not an object in all this? Did I believe as you do, I should say that it was Heaven working in us—no: do not answer that the working comes from lower down. I take no credit for reading that upon your lips; the retort is too easy and obvious. I am content to say, however, that the work is that of instinct and nature, or, if you will, of fate, pointing out a road by which together we might travel to great ends."

"I travel my road alone, Mr. Meyer."

"I know, I know, and that is the pity of it. The trouble between man and woman is that not in one case out of a million, even if they be lovers, do they understand each other. Their eyes may seek one another, their hands and lips may meet, and yet they remain distinct, apart, and often antagonistic. There is no communication of the soul. But when it chances to be hewn from the same rock as it were—oh! then what happiness may be theirs, and what opportunities!"

"Possibly, Mr. Meyer; but, to be frank, the question does not interest me."

"Not yet; but I am sure that one day it will. Meanwhile, I owe you an apology. I lost my temper before you last night. Well, do not judge me hardly, for I was utterly worn out, and that old idiot vexed me with his talk about ghosts, in which I do not believe."

"Then why did it make you so angry? Surely you could have afforded to treat it with contempt, instead of doing—as you did."

"Upon my word! I don't know, but I suppose most of us are afraid lest we should be forced to accept that which we refuse. This ancient place gets upon the nerves, Miss Clifford; yours as well as mine. I can afford to be open about it, because I know that you know. Think of its associations: all the crime that has been committed here for ages and ages, all the suffering that has been endured here. Doubtless human sacrifices were offered in this cave or outside of it; that great burnt ring in the rock there may have been where they built the fires. And then those Portuguese starving to death, slowly starving to death while thousands of savages watched them die. Have you ever thought what it means? But of course you have, for like myself you are cursed with imagination. God in heaven! is it wonderful that it gets upon the nerves? especially when one cannot find what one is looking for, that vast treasure"—and his face became ecstatic—"that shall yet be yours and mine, and make us great and happy."

"But which at present only makes me a scullery-maid and most unhappy," replied Benita cheerfully, for she heard her father's footstep. "Don't talk any more of the treasure, Mr. Meyer, or we shall quarrel. We have enough of that during business hours, when we are hunting for it, you know. Give me the dish, will you? This meat is cooked at last."

Still Benita could not be rid of that treasure, since after breakfast the endless, unprofitable search began again. Once more the cave was sounded, and other hollow places were discovered upon which the two men got to work. With infinite labour three of them were broken into in as many days, and like the first, found to be graves, only this time of ancients who, perhaps, had died before Christ was born. There they lay upon their sides, their bones burnt by the hot cement that had been poured over them, their gold-headed and gold-ferruled rods of office in their hands, their gold-covered pillows of wood, such as the Egyptians used, beneath their skulls, gold bracelets upon their arms and ankles, cakes of gold beneath them which had fallen from the rotted pouches that once hung about their waists, vases of fine glazed pottery that had been filled with offerings, or in some cases with gold dust to pay the expenses of their journey in the other world, standing round them, and so forth.

In their way these discoveries were rich enough—from one tomb alone they took over a hundred and thirty ounces of gold—to say nothing of their surpassing archæological interest. Still they were not what they sought: all that gathered wealth of Monomotapa which the fleeing Portuguese had brought with them and buried in this, their last stronghold.

Benita ceased to take the slightest interest in the matter; she would not even be at the pains to go to look at the third skeleton, although it was that of a man who had been almost a giant, and, to judge from the amount of bullion which he took to the tomb with him, a person of great importance in his day. She felt as though she wished never to see another human bone or ancient bead or bangle; the sight of a street in Bayswater in a London fog—yes, or a toy-shop window in Westbourne Grove—would have pleased her a hundred times better than these unique remains that, had they known of them in those days, would have sent half the learned societies of Europe crazy with delight. She wished to escape from Bambatse, its wondrous fortifications, its mysterious cone, its cave, its dead, and—from Jacob Meyer.

Benita stood upon the top of her prison wall and looked with longing at the wide, open lands below. She even dared to climb the stairs which ran up the mighty cone of granite, and seated herself in the cup-like depression on its crest, whence Jacob Meyer had called to her to come and share his throne. It was a dizzy place, for the pillar leaning outwards, its point stood almost clear of the water-scarped rock, so that beneath her was a sheer drop of about four hundred feet to the Zambesi bed. At first the great height made her feel faint. Her eyes swam, and unpleasant tremors crept along her spine, so that she was glad to sink to the floor, whence she knew she could not fall. By degrees, however, she recovered her nerve, and was able to study the glorious view of stream and marshes and hills beyond.

For she had come here with a purpose, to see whether it would not be possible to escape down the river in a canoe, or in native boats such as the Makalanga owned and used for fishing, or to cross from bank to bank. Apparently it was impossible, for although the river beneath and above them was still enough, about a mile below began a cataract that stretched as far as she could see, and was bordered on either side by rocky hills covered with forest, over which, even if they could obtain porters, a canoe could not be carried. This, indeed, she had already heard from the Molimo, but knowing his timid nature, she wished to judge of the matter for herself. It came to this then: if they were to go, it must be on the horses.

Descending the cone Benita went to find her father, to whom as yet she had said nothing of her plans. The opportunity was good, for she knew that he would be alone. As it chanced, on that afternoon Meyer had gone down the hill in order to try to persuade the Makalanga to give them ten or twenty men to help them in their excavations. In this, it will be remembered, he had already failed so far as the Molimo was concerned, but he was not a man easily turned from his purpose, and he thought that if he could see Tamas and some of the other captains he might be able by bribery, threats, or otherwise, to induce them to forget their superstitious fears, and help in the search. As a matter of fact, he was utterly unsuccessful, since one and all they declared that for them to enter that sacred place would mean their deaths, and that the vengeance of Heaven would fall upon their tribe and destroy it root and branch.

Mr. Clifford, on whom all this heavy labour had begun to tell, was taking advantage of the absence of his taskmaster, Jacob, to sleep awhile in the hut which they had now built for themselves beneath the shadow of the baobab-tree. As she reached it he came out yawning, and asked her where she had been. Benita told him.

"A giddy place," he said. "I have never ventured to try it myself. What did you go up there for, dear?"

"To look at the river while Mr. Meyer was away, father; for if he had seen me do so he would have guessed my reason; indeed, I dare say that he will guess it now."

"What reason, Benita?"

"To see whether it would not be possible to escape down it in a boat. But there is no chance. It is all rapids below, with hills and rocks and trees on either bank."

"What need have you to escape at present?" he asked, eyeing her curiously.

"Every need," she answered with passion. "I hate this place; it is a prison, and I loathe the very name of treasure. Also," and she paused.

"Also what, dear?"

"Also," and her voice sank to a whisper, as though she feared that he should overhear her even at the bottom of the hill; "also, I am afraid of Mr. Meyer."

This confession did not seem to surprise her father, who merely nodded his head and said:

"Go on."

"Father, I think that he is going mad, and it is not pleasant for us to be cooped up here alone with a madman, especially when he has begun to speak to me as he does now."

"You don't mean that he has been impertinent to you," said the old man, flushing up, "for if so— —"

"No, not impertinent—as yet," and she told him what had passed between Meyer and herself, adding, "You see, father, I detest this man; indeed, I want to have nothing to do with any man; for me all that is over and done with," and she gave a dry little sob which appeared to come from her very heart. "And yet, he seems to be getting some kind of power over me. He follows me about with his eyes, prying into my mind, and I feel that he is beginning to be able to read it. I can bear no more. Father, father, for God's sake, take me away from this hateful hill and its gold and its dead, and let us get out into the veld again together."

"I should be glad enough, dearest," he answered. "I have had plenty of this wild-goose chase, which I was so mad as to be led into by the love of wealth. Indeed, I am beginning to believe that if it goes on much longer I shall leave my bones here."

"And if such a dreadful thing as that were to happen, what would become of me, alone with Jacob Meyer?" she asked quietly. "I might even be driven to the same fate as that poor girl two hundred years ago," and she pointed to the cone of rock behind her.

"For Heaven's sake, don't talk like that!" he broke in.

"Why not? One must face things, and it would be better than Jacob Meyer; for who would protect me here?"

Mr. Clifford walked up and down for a few minutes, while his daughter watched him anxiously.

"I can see no plan," he said, stopping opposite her. "We cannot take the waggon even if there are enough oxen left to draw it, for it is his as much as mine, and I am sure that he will never leave this treasure unless he is driven away."

"And I am sure I hope that he will not. But, father, the horses are our own; it was his that died, you remember. We can ride away on them."

He stared at her and answered:

"Yes, we could ride away to our deaths. Suppose they got sick or lame; suppose we meet the Matabele, or could find no game to shoot; suppose one of us fell ill—oh! and a hundred things. What then?"

"Why, then it is just as well to perish in the wilderness as here, where our risks are almost as great. We must take our chance, and trust to God. Perhaps He will be merciful and help us. Listen now, father. To-morrow is Sunday, when you and I do no work that we can help. Mr. Meyer is a Jew, and he won't waste Sunday. Well now, I will say that I want to go down to the outer wall to fetch some clothes which I left in the waggon, and to take others for the native women to wash, and of course you will come with me. Perhaps he will be deceived, and stay behind, especially as he has been there to-day. Then we can get the horses and guns and ammunition, and anything else that we can carry in the way of food, and persuade the old Molimo to open the gate for us. You know, the little side gate that cannot be seen from up here, and before Mr. Meyer misses us and comes to look, we shall be twenty miles away, and—horses can't be overtaken by a man on foot."

"He will say that we have deserted him, and that will be true."

"You can leave a letter with the Molimo explaining that it was my fault, that I was getting ill and thought that I should die, and that you knew it would not be fair to ask him to come, and so to lose the treasure, to every halfpenny of which he is welcome when it is found. Oh! father, don't hesitate any longer; say that you will take me away from Mr. Meyer."

"So be it then," answered Mr. Clifford, and as he spoke, hearing a sound, they looked up and saw Jacob approaching them.

Luckily he was so occupied with his own thoughts that he never noted the guilty air upon their faces, and they had time to compose themselves a little. But even thus his suspicions were aroused.

"What are you talking of so earnestly?" he asked.

"We were wondering how you were getting on with the Makalanga," answered Benita, fibbing boldly, "and whether you would persuade them to face the ghosts. Did you?"

"Not I," he answered with a scowl. "Those ghosts are our worst enemies in this place; the cowards swore that they would rather die. I should have liked to take some of them at their word and make ghosts of them; but I remembered the situation and didn't. Don't be afraid, Miss Clifford, I never even lost my temper, outwardly at any rate. Well, there it is; if they won't help us, we must work the harder. I've got a new plan, and we'll begin on it to-morrow."

"Not to-morrow, Mr. Meyer," replied Benita with a smile. "It is Sunday, and we rest on Sunday, you know."

"Oh! I forgot. The Makalanga with their ghosts and you with your Sunday—really I do not know which is the worse. Well, then, I must do my own share and yours too, I suppose," and he turned with a shrug of his shoulders.

XIV.
THE FLIGHT

The next morning, Sunday, Meyer went to work on his new plan. What it was Benita did not trouble to inquire, but she gathered that it had something to do with the measuring out of the chapel cave into squares for the more systematic investigation of each area. At twelve o'clock he emerged for his midday meal, in the course of which he remarked that it was very dreary working in that place alone, and that he would be glad when it was Monday, and they could accompany him. His words evidently disturbed Mr. Clifford not a little, and even excited some compunction in the breast of Benita.

What would his feelings be, she wondered, when he found that they had run away, leaving him to deal with their joint undertaking single-handed! Almost was she minded to tell him the whole truth; yet—and this was a curious evidence of the man's ascendancy over her—she did not. Perhaps she felt that to do so would be to put an end to their scheme, since then by argument, blandishments, threats, force, or appeal to their sense of loyalty, it mattered not which, he would bring about its abandonment. But she wanted to fulfil that scheme, to be free of Bambatse, its immemorial ruins, its graveyard cave, and the ghoul, Jacob Meyer, who could delve among dead bones and in living hearts with equal skill and insight, and yet was unable to find the treasure that lay beneath either of them.

So they hid the truth, and talked with feverish activity about other things, such as the drilling of the Makalanga, and the chances of an attack by the Matabele, which happily now seemed to be growing small; also of the conditions of their cattle, and the prospect of obtaining more to replace those that had died. Indeed, Benita went farther; in her new-found zeal of deception she proceeded to act a lie, yes, even with her father's reproachful eyes fixed upon her. Incidentally she mentioned that they were going to have an outing, to climb down the ladder and visit the Makalanga camp between the first and second walls and mix with the great world for a few hours; also to carry their washing to be done there, and bring up some clean clothes and certain books which she had left below.

Jacob came out of his thoughts and calculations, and listened gloomily.

"I have half a mind to come with you," he said, words at which Benita shivered. "It certainly is most cursed lonesome in that cave, and I seem to hear things in it, as though those old bones were rattling, sounds like sighs and whispers too, which are made by the draught."

"Well, why don't you?" asked Benita.

It was a bold stroke, but it succeeded. If he had any doubts they vanished, and he answered at once:

"Because I have not the time. We have to get this business finished one way or another before the wet season comes on, and we are drowned out of the place with rain, or rotted by fever. Take your afternoon out, Miss Clifford; every maid of all work is entitled to as much, and I am afraid that is your billet here. Only," he added, with that care for her safety which he always showed in his more temperate moods, "pray be careful, Clifford, to get back before sundown. That wall is too risky for your daughter to climb in the dusk. Call me from the foot of it; you have the whistle, and I will come down to help her up. I think I'll go with you after all. No, I won't. I made myself so unpleasant to them yesterday that those Makalanga can't wish to see any more of me at present. I hope you will have a more agreeable afternoon than I shall. Why don't you take a ride outside the wall? Your horses are fat and want exercise, and I do not think that you need be afraid of the Matabele." Then without waiting for an answer, he rose and left them.

Mr. Clifford looked after him doubtfully.

"Oh, I know," said Benita, "it seems horribly mean, but one must do shabby things sometimes. Here are the bundles all ready, so let us be off."

Accordingly they went, and from the top of the wall Benita glanced back to bid goodbye to that place which she hoped never to see again. Yet she could not feel as though she looked her last upon it; to her it wore no air of farewell, and even as she descended the perilous stairs, she found herself making mental notes as to how they might best be climbed again. Also, she could not believe that she had done with Mr. Meyer. It seemed to her as though for a long while yet her future would be full of him.

They reached the outer fortifications in safety, and there were greeted with some surprise but with no displeasure by the Makalanga, whom they found still drilling with the rifles, in the use of which a certain number of them appeared to have become fairly proficient. Going to the hut in which the spare goods from the waggon had been stored, they quickly made their preparations. Here also, Mr. Clifford wrote a letter, one of the most unpleasant that he had ever been called upon to compose. It ran thus:

"Dear Meyer,

"I don't know what you will think of us, but we are escaping from this place. The truth is that I am not well, and my daughter can bear it no longer. She says that if she stops here, she will die, and that hunting for treasure in that ghastly grave-yard is shattering her nerves. I should have liked to tell you, but she begged me not, being convinced that if I did, you would over-persuade us or stop us in some way. As for the gold, if you can find it, take it all. I renounce my share. We are leaving you the waggon and the oxen, and starting down country on our horses. It is a perilous business, but less so than staying here, under the circumstances. If we never meet again we hope that you will forgive us, and wish you all good fortune.—Yours sincerely and with much regret,

"T. Clifford."

The letter written, they saddled the horses which had been brought up for their inspection, and were found to be in good case, and fastened their scanty belongings, and as many cartridges as they could carry in packs behind their saddles. Then, each of them armed with a rifle—for during their long journeyings Benita had learned to shoot—they mounted and made for the little side-entrance, as the main gate through which they had passed on their arrival was now built up. This side-entrance, a mere slit in the great wall, with a precipitous approach, was open, for now that their fear of the Matabele had to some extent passed off, the Makalanga used it to drive their sheep and goats in and out, since it was so constructed with several twists and turns in the thickness of the wall, that in a few minutes it could be effectually blocked by stones that lay at hand. Also, the ancient architect had arranged it in such a fashion that it was entirely commanded from the crest of the wall on either side.

The Makalanga, who had been watching their proceedings curiously, made no attempt to stop them, although they guessed that they might have a little trouble with the sentries who guarded the entrances all day, and even when it was closed at night, with whom also Mr. Clifford proposed to leave the letter. When they reached the place, however, and had dismounted to lead the horses down the winding passage and the steep ascent upon its further side, it was to find that the only guard visible proved to be the old Molimo himself, who sat there, apparently half asleep.

But as they came he showed himself to be very much awake, for without moving he asked them at once whither they were going.

"To take a ride," answered Mr. Clifford. "The lady, my daughter, is weary of being cooped up in this fortress, and wishes to breathe the air without. Let us pass, friend, or we shall not be back by sunset."

"If you be coming back at sunset, white man, why do you carry so many things upon your packs, and why are your saddle-bags filled with cartridges?" he asked. "Surely you do not speak the truth to me, and you hope that never more will you see the sun set upon Bambatse."

Now understanding that it was hopeless to deceive him, Benita exclaimed boldly:

"It is so; but oh! my Father, stay us not, for fear is behind us, and therefore we fly hence."

"And is there no fear before you, maiden? Fear of the wilderness, where none wander save perchance the Amandabele with their bloody spears; fear of wild beasts and of sickness that may overtake you so that, first one and then the other, you perish there?"

"There is plenty, my Father, but none of them so bad as the fear behind. Yonder place is haunted, and we give up our search and would dwell there no more."

"It is haunted truly, maiden, but its spirits will not harm you whom they welcome as one appointed, and we are ever ready to protect you because of their command that has come to me in dreams. Nor, indeed, is it the spirits whom you fear, but rather the white man, your companion, who would bend you to his will. Deny it not, for I have seen it all."

"Then knowing the truth, surely you will let us go," she pleaded, "for I swear to you that I dare not stay."

"Who am I that I should forbid you?" he asked. "Yet I tell you that you would do well to stay and save yourselves much terror. Maiden, have I not said it days and days ago, that here and here only you must accomplish your fate? Go now if you will, but you shall return again," and once more he seemed to begin to doze in the sun.

The two of them consulted hastily together.

"It is no use turning back now," said Benita, who was almost weeping with doubt and vexation. "I will not be frightened by his vague talk. What can he know of the future more than any of the rest of us? Besides, all he says is that we shall come back again, and if that does happen, at least we shall have been free for a little while. Come, father."

"As you wish," answered Mr. Clifford, who seemed too miserable and depressed to argue. Only he threw down the letter upon the Molimo's lap, and begged him to give it to Meyer when he came to look for them.

The old man took no notice; no, not even when Benita bade him farewell and thanked him for his kindness, praying that all good fortune might attend him and his tribe, did he answer a single word or even look up. So they led their horses down the narrow passage where there was scarcely room for them to pass, and up the steep path beyond. On the further side of the ancient ditch they remounted them while the Makalanga watched them from the walls, and cantered away along the same road by which they had come.

Now this road, or rather track, ran first through the gardens and then among the countless ruined houses that in bygone ages formed the great city whereof the mount Bambatse had been the citadel and sanctuary. The relics of a lost civilization extended for several miles, and were bounded by a steep and narrow neck or pass in the encircling hills, the same that Robert Seymour and his brother had found too difficult for their waggon at the season in which they visited the place some years before. This pass, or port as it is called in South Africa, had been strongly fortified, for on either side of it were the ruins of towers. Moreover, at its crest it was so narrow and steep-sided that a few men posted there, even if they were armed only with bows and arrows, could hold an attacking force in check for a considerable time. Beyond it, after the hill was descended, a bush-clad plain dotted with kopjes and isolated granite pillars formed of boulders piled one upon another, rolled away for many miles.

Mr. Clifford and Benita had started upon their mad journey about three o'clock in the afternoon, and when the sun began to set they found themselves upon this plain fifteen or sixteen miles from Bambatse, of which they had long lost sight, for it lay beyond the intervening hills. Near to them was a kopje, where they had outspanned by a spring of water when on their recent journey, and since they did not dare to travel in the dark, here they determined to off-saddle, for round this spring was good grass for the horses.

As it chanced, they came upon some hartebeeste here which were trekking down to drink, but although they would have been glad of meat, they were afraid to shoot, fearing lest they should attract attention; nor for the same reason did they like to light a fire. So having knee-haltered the horses in such fashion that they could not wander far, and turned them loose to feed, they sat down under a tree, and made some sort of a meal off the biltong and cooked corn which they had brought with them. By the time this was finished darkness fell, for there was little moon, so that nothing remained to do except to sleep within a circle of a few dead thorn-boughs which they had drawn about their camp. This, then, they did, and so weary were they both, that notwithstanding all the emotions through which they had passed, and their fears lest lions should attack them—for of these brutes there were many in this veld—rested soundly and undisturbed till within half an hour of dawn.

Rising somewhat chilled, for though the air was warm a heavy dew had soaked their blankets, once more they ate and drank by starlight, while the horses, which they had tied up close to them during the night, filled themselves with grass. At the first break of day they saddled them, and before the sun rose were on their road again. At length up it came, and the sight and warmth of it put new heart into Benita. Her fears seemed to depart with the night, and she said to her father that this successful start was of good augury, to which he only answered that he hoped so.

All that day they rode forward in beautiful weather, not pressing their horses, for now they were sure that Jacob Meyer, who if he followed at all must do so on foot, would never be able to overtake them. At noon they halted, and having shot a small buck, Benita cooked some of it in the one pot that they had brought with them, and they ate a good meal of fresh meat.

Riding on again, towards sundown they came to another of their old camping-places, also a bush-covered kopje. Here the spring of water was more than halfway up the hill, so there they off-saddled in a green bower of a place that because of its ferns and mosses looked like a rock garden. Now, although they had enough cold meat for food, they thought themselves quite safe in lighting a fire. Indeed, this it seemed necessary to do, since they had struck the fresh spoor of lions, and even caught sight of one galloping away in the tall reeds on the marshy land at the foot of the hill.

That evening they fared sumptuously upon venison, and as on the previous day lay down to rest in a little "boma" or fence made of boughs. But they were not allowed to sleep well this night, for scarcely had they shut their eyes when a hyena began to howl about them. They shouted and the brute went away, but an hour or two later, they heard ominous grunting sounds, followed presently by a loud roar, which was answered by another roar, whereat the horses began to whinny in a frightened fashion.

"Lions!" said Mr. Clifford, jumping up and throwing dead wood on the fire till it burnt to a bright blaze.

After that all sleep became impossible, for although the lions did not attack them, having once winded the horses they would not go away, but continued wandering round the kopje, grunting and growling. This went on till abut three o'clock in the morning, when at last the beasts took their departure, for they heard them roaring in the distance. Now that they seemed safe, having first made up the fire, they tried to get some rest.

When, as it appeared to her, Benita had been asleep but a little while, she was awakened by a new noise. It was still dark, but the starlight showed her that the horses were quite quiet; indeed, one of them was lying down, and the other eating some green leaves from the branches of the tree to which it was tethered. Therefore that noise had not come from any wild animal of which they were afraid. She listened intently, and presently heard it again; it was a murmur like to that of people talking somewhere at the bottom of the hill. Then she woke her father and told him, but although once or twice they thought they heard the sound of footsteps, nothing else could be distinguished. Still they rose, and having saddled and bridled the horses as noiselessly as might be, waited for the dawn.

At last it came. Up on the side of the kopje they were in clear air, above which shone the red lights of morning, but under them lay billows of dense, pearl-hued mist. By degrees this thinned beneath the rays of the risen sun, and through it, looking gigantic in that light, Benita saw a savage wrapped in a kaross, who was walking up and down and yawning, a great spear in his hand.

"Look," she whispered, "look!" and Mr. Clifford stared down the line of her outstretched finger.

"The Matabele," he said. "My God! the Matabele!"

XV.
THE CHASE

The Matabele it was, sure enough; there could be no doubt of it, for soon three other men joined the sentry and began to talk with him, pointing with their great spears at the side of the hill. Evidently they were arranging a surprise when there was sufficient light to carry it out.

"They have seen our fire," whispered her father to Benita; "now, if we wish to save our lives, there is only one thing to do—ride for it before they muster. The impi will be camped upon the other side of the hill, so we must take the road we came by."

"That runs back to Bambatse," faltered Benita.

"Bambatse is better than the grave," said her father. "Pray Heaven that we may get there."

To this argument there was no answer, so having drunk a sup of water, and swallowing a few mouthfuls of food as they went, they crept to the horses, mounted them, and as silently as possible began to ride down the hill.

The sentry was alone again, the other three men having departed. He stood with his back towards them. Presently when they were quite close on to him, he heard their horses' hoofs upon the grass, wheeled round at the sound, and saw them. Then with a great shout he lifted his spear and charged.

Mr. Clifford, who was leading, held out his rifle at arm's length— to raise it to his shoulder he had no time—and pulled the trigger. Benita heard the bullet clap upon the hide shield, and next instant saw the Matabele warrior lying on his back, beating the air with his hands and feet. Also, she saw beyond the shoulder of the kopje, which they were rounding, hundreds of men marching, and behind them a herd of cattle, the dim light gleaming upon the stabbing spears and on the horns of the oxen. She glanced to the right, and there were more men.

The two wings of the impi were closing upon them. Only a little lane was left in the middle. They must get through before it shut.

"Come," she gasped, striking the horse with her heel and the butt of her gun, and jerking at its mouth.

Her father saw also, and did likewise, so that the beasts broke into a gallop. Now from the point of each wing sprang out thin lines of men, looking like great horns, or nippers, whose business it was to meet and cut them off. Could they pass between them before they did meet? That was the question, and upon its answer it depended whether or no they had another three minutes to live. To think of mercy at the hands of these bloodthirsty brutes, after they had just killed one of their number before their eyes, was absurd. It was true he had been shot in self-defence; but what count would savages take of that, or of the fact that they were but harmless travellers? White people were not very popular with the Matabele just then, as they knew well; also, their murder in this remote place, with not another of their race within a couple of hundred miles, would never even be reported, and much less avenged. It was as safe as any crime could possibly be.

All this passed through their minds as they galloped towards those closing points. Oh! the horror of it! But two hundred yards to cover, and their fate would be decided. Either they would have escaped at least for a while, or time would be done with them; or, a third alternative, they might be taken prisoners, in all probability a yet more dreadful doom. Even then Benita determined that if she could help it this should not befall her. She had the rifle and the revolver that Jacob Meyer had given her. Surely she would be able to find a moment to use one or the other upon herself. She clenched her teeth, and struck the horse again and again, so that now they flew along. The Matabele soldiers were running their best to catch them, and if these had been given but five seconds of start, caught they must have been. But that short five seconds saved their lives.

When they rushed through them the foremost men of the nippers were not more than twenty yards apart. Seeing that they had passed, these halted and hurled a shower of spears after them. One flashed by Benita's cheek, a line of light; she felt the wind of it. Another cut her dress, and a third struck her father's horse in the near hind leg just above the knee-joint, remaining fast there for a stride or two, and then falling to the ground. At first the beast did not seem to be incommoded by this wound; indeed, it only caused it to gallop quicker, and Benita rejoiced, thinking that it was but a scratch. Then she forgot about it, for some of the Matabele, who had guns, began to shoot them, and although their marksmanship was vile, one or two of the bullets went nearer than was pleasant. Lastly a man, the swiftest runner of them all, shouted after them in Zulu:

"The horse is wounded. We will catch you both before the sun sets."

Then they passed over the crest of a rise and lost sight of them for a while.

"Thank God!" gasped Benita when they were alone again in the silent veld; but Mr. Clifford shook his head.

"Do you think they will follow us?" she asked.

"You heard what the fellow said," he answered evasively. "Doubtless they are on their way to attack Bambatse, and have been round to destroy some other wretched tribe, and steal the cattle which we saw. Yes, I fear that they will follow. The question is, which of us can get to Bambatse first."

"Surely we ought to on the horses, father."

"Yes, if nothing happens to them," and as he spoke the words the mare which he was riding dropped sharply upon her hind leg, the same that had been struck with the spear; then recovered herself and galloped on.

"Did you see that?" he asked.

She nodded; then said:

"Shall we get off and look at the cut?"

"Certainly not," he answered. "Our only chance is to keep her moving; if once the wound stiffens, there's an end. The sinew cannot have been severed, or it would have come before now."

So they pushed on.

All that morning did they canter forward wherever the ground was smooth enough to allow them to do so, and notwithstanding the increasing lameness of Mr. Clifford's mare, made such good progress that by midday they reached the place where they had passed the first night after leaving Bambatse. Here sheer fatigue and want of water forced them to stop a little while. They dismounted and drank greedily from the spring, after which they allowed the horses to drink also; indeed it was impossible to keep them away from the water. Then they ate a little, not because they desired food, but to keep up their strength, and while they did so examined the mare. By now her hind leg was much swollen, and blood still ran from the gash made by the assegai. Moreover, the limb was drawn up so that the point of the hoof only rested on the ground.

"We must get on before it sets fast," said Mr. Clifford, and they mounted again.

Great heavens! what was this? The mare would not stir. In his despair Mr. Clifford beat it cruelly, whereupon the poor brute hobbled forward a few paces on three legs, and again came to a standstill. Either an injured sinew had given or the inflammation was now so intense that it could not bend its knee. Understanding what this meant to them, Benita's nerve gave out at last, and she burst into weeping.

"Don't cry, love," he said. "God's will be done. Perhaps they have given up the hunt by now; at any rate, my legs are left, and Bambatse is not more than sixteen miles away. Forward now," and holding to her saddle-strap they went up the long, long slope which led to the poort in the hills around Bambatse.

They would have liked to shoot the mare, but being afraid to fire a rifle, could not do so. So they left the unhappy beast to its fate, and with it everything it carried, except a few of the cartridges. Before they went, however, at Benita's prayer, her father devoted a few seconds to unbuckling the girths and pulling off the bridle, so that it might have a chance of life. For a little way it hobbled after them on three legs, then, the saddle still upon its back, stood whinnying piteously, till at last, to Benita's intense relief, a turn in their path hid it from their sight.

Half a mile further on she looked round in the faint hope that it might have recovered itself and followed. But no mare was to be seen. Something else was to be seen, however, for there, three or four miles away upon the plain behind them, easy to be distinguished in that dazzling air, were a number of black spots that occasionally seemed to sparkle.

"What are they?" she asked faintly, as one who feared the answer.

"The Matabele who follow us," answered her father, "or rather a company of their swiftest runners. It is their spears that glitter so. Now, my love, this is the position," he went on, as they struggled forward: "those men will catch us before ever we can get to Bambatse; they are trained to run like that, for fifty miles, if need be. But with this start they cannot catch your horse, you must go on and leave me to look after myself."

"Never, never!" she exclaimed.

"But you shall, and you must. I am your father and I order you. As for me, what does it matter? I may hide from them and escape, or—at least I am old, my life is done, whereas yours is before you. Now, good-bye, and go on," and he let go of the saddle-strap.

By way of answer Benita pulled up the horse.

"Not one yard," she said, setting her mouth.

Then he began to storm at her, calling her disobedient, and undutiful, and when this means failed to move her, to implore her almost with tears.

"Father, dear," she said, leaning down towards him as he walked, for now they were going on again, "I told you why I wanted to run away from Bambatse, didn't I?—because I would rather risk my life than stay. Well, do you think that I wish to return there and live in that place alone with Jacob Meyer? Also, I will tell you another thing. You remember about Mr. Seymour? Well, I can't get over that; I can't get over it at all, and therefore, although of course I am afraid, it is all one to me. No, we will escape together, or die together; the first if we can."

Then with a groan he gave up the argument, and as he found breath they discussed their chances. Their first idea was to hide, but save for a few trees all the country was open; there was no place to cover them. They thought of the banks of the Zambesi, but between them and the river rose a bare, rock-strewn hill with several miles of slope. Long before they could reach its crest, even if a horse were able to travel there, they must be overtaken. In short, there was nothing to do except to push for the nek, and if they were fortunate enough to reach it before the Matabele, to abandon the horse there and try to conceal themselves among the ruins of the houses beyond. This, perhaps, they might do when once the sun was down.

But they did not deceive themselves; the chances were at least fifty to one against them, unless indeed their pursuers grew weary and let them go.

At present, however, they were by no means weary, for having perceived them from far away, the long-legged runners put on the pace, and the distance between them and their quarry was lessening.

"Father," said Benita, "please understand one thing. I do not mean to be taken alive by those savages."

"Oh! how can I — —" he faltered.

"I don't ask you," she answered. "I will see to that myself. Only, if I should make any mistake— —" and she looked at him.

The old man was getting very tired. He panted up the steep hillside, and stumbled against the stones. Benita noted it, and slipping from the horse, made him mount while she ran alongside. Then when he was a little rested they changed places again, and so covered several miles of country. Subsequently, when both of them were nearly exhausted, they tried riding together—she in front and he behind, for their baggage had long since been thrown away. But the weary beast could not carry this double burden, and after a few hundred yards of it, stumbled, fell, struggled to its feet again, and stopped.

So once more they were obliged to ride and walk alternately.

Now there was not much more than an hour of daylight left, and the narrow pass lay about three miles ahead of them. That dreadful three miles; ever thereafter it was Benita's favourite nightmare! At the beginning of it the leading Matabele were about two thousand yards behind them; half-way, about a thousand; and at the commencement of the last mile, say five hundred.

Nature is a wonderful thing, and great are its resources in extremity. As the actual crisis approached, the weariness of these two seemed to depart, or at any rate it was forgotten. They no longer felt exhausted, nor, had they been fresh from their beds, could they have climbed or run better. Even the horse seemed to find new energy, and when it lagged Mr. Clifford dug the point of his hunting knife into its flank. Gasping, panting, now one mounted and now the other, they struggled on towards that crest of rock, while behind them came death in the shape of those sleuth-hounds of Matabele. The sun was going down, and against its flaming ball, when they glanced back they could see their dark forms outlined; the broad spears also looked red as though they had been dipped in blood. They could even hear their taunting shouts as they called to them to sit down and be killed, and save trouble.

Now they were not three hundred yards away, and the crest of the pass was still half a mile ahead. Five minutes passed, and here, where the track was very rough, the horse blundered upwards slowly. Mr. Clifford was riding at the time, and Benita running at his side, holding to the stirrup leather. She looked behind her. The savages, fearing that their victims might find shelter over the hill, were making a rush, and the horse could go no faster. One man, a great tall fellow, quite outdistanced his companions. Two minutes more and he was not over a hundred paces from them, a little nearer than they were to the top of the pass. Then the horse stopped and refused to stir any more.

Mr. Clifford jumped from the saddle, and Benita, who could not speak, pointed to the pursuing Matabele. He sat down upon a rock, cocked his rifle, took a deep breath, and aimed and fired at the soldier who was coming on carelessly in the open. Mr. Clifford was a good shot, and shaken though he was, at this supreme moment his skill did not fail him. The man was struck somewhere, for he staggered about and fell; then slowly picked himself up, and began to hobble back towards his companions, who, when they met him, stopped a minute to give him some kind of assistance.

That halt proved their salvation, for it gave them time to make one last despairing rush, and gain the brow of the poort. Not that this would have saved them, however, since where they could go the Matabele could follow, and there was still light by which the pursuers would have been able to see to catch them. Indeed, the savages, having laid down the wounded man, came on with a yell of rage, fifty or more of them.

Over the pass father and daughter struggled, Benita riding; after them, perhaps sixty yards away, ran the Matabele, gathered in a knot now upon the narrow, ancient road, bordered by steep hillsides.

Then suddenly from all about them, as it appeared to Benita, broke out the blaze and roar of rifles, rapid and continuous. Down went the Matabele by twos and threes, till at last it seemed as though but quite a few of them were left upon their feet, and those came on no more; they turned and fled from the neck of the narrow pass to the open slope beyond.

Benita sank to the ground, and the next thing that she could remember was hearing the soft voice of Jacob Meyer, who said:

"So you have returned from your ride, Miss Clifford, and perhaps it was as well that the thought came from you to me that you wished me to meet you here in this very place."

XVI.
BACK AT BAMBATSE

How they reached Bambatse Benita never could remember, but afterwards she was told that both she and her father were carried upon litters made of ox-hide shields. When she came to her own mind again, it was to find herself lying in her tent outside the mouth of the cave within the third enclosure of the temple-fortress. Her feet were sore and her bones ached, physical discomforts that brought back to her in a flash all the terrors through which she had passed.

Again she saw the fierce pursuing Matabele; again heard their cruel shouts and the answering crack of the rifles; again, amidst the din and the gathering darkness, distinguished the gentle, foreign voice of Meyer speaking his words of sarcastic greeting. Next oblivion fell upon her, and after it a dim memory of being helped up the hill with the sun pouring on her back and assisted to climb the steep steps of the wall by means of a rope placed around her. Then forgetfulness again.

The flap of her tent was drawn aside and she shrank back upon her bed, shutting her eyes for fear lest they should fall upon the face of Jacob Meyer. Feeling that it was not he, or learning it perhaps from the footfall, she opened them a little, peeping at her visitor from between her long lashes. He proved to be—not Jacob or her father, but the old Molimo, who stood beside her holding in his hand a gourd filled with goat's milk. Then she sat up and smiled at him, for Benita had grown very fond of this ancient man, who was so unlike anyone that she had ever met.

"Greeting, Lady," he said softly, smiling back at her with his lips and dreamy eyes, for his old face did not seem to move beneath its thousand wrinkles. "I bring you milk. Drink; it is fresh and you need food."

So she took the gourd and drank to the last drop, for it seemed to her that she had never tasted anything so delicious.

"Good, good," murmured the Molimo; "now you will be well again."

"Yes, I shall get well," she answered; "but oh! what of my father?"

"Fear not; he is still sick, but he will recover also. You shall see him soon."

"I have drunk all the milk," she broke out; "there is none left for him."

"Plenty, plenty," he answered, waving his thin hand. "There are two cups full—one for each. We have not many she-goats down below, but the best of their milk is saved for you."

"Tell me all that has happened, Father," and the old priest, who liked her to call him by that name, smiled again with his eyes, and squatted down in the corner of the tent.

"You went away, you remember that you would go, although I told you that you must come back. You refused my wisdom and you went, and I have learned all that befell you and how you two escaped the impi. Well, that night after sunset, when you did not return, came the Black One—yes, yes, I mean Meyer, whom we name so because of his beard, and," he added deliberately, "his heart. He came running down the hill asking for you, and I gave him the letter.

"He read it, and oh! then he went mad. He cursed in his own tongue; he threw himself about; he took a rifle and wished to shoot me, but I sat silent and looked at him till he grew quiet. Then he asked why I had played him this trick, but I answered that it was no trick of mine who had no right to keep you and your father prisoners against your will, and that I thought you had gone away because you were afraid of him, which was not wonderful if that was how he talked to you. I told him, too, I who am a doctor, that unless he was careful he would go mad; that already I saw madness in his eye; after which he became quiet, for my words frightened him. Then he asked what could be done, and I said—that night, nothing, since you must be far away, so that it would be useless to follow you, but better to go to meet you when you came back. He asked what I meant by your coming back, and I answered that I meant what I said, that you would come back in great haste and peril—although you would not believe me when I told you so—for I had it from the Munwali whose child you are.

"So I sent out my spies, and that night went by, and the next day and night went by, and we sat still and did nothing, though the Black One wished to wander out alone after you. But on the following morning, at the dawn, a messenger came in who reported that it had been called to him by his brethren who were hidden upon hilltops and in other places for miles and miles, that the Matabele impi, having destroyed another family of the Makalanga far down the Zambesi, was advancing to destroy us also. And in the afternoon came a second spy, who reported that you two had been surrounded by the impi, but had broken through them, and were riding hitherward for your lives. Then I took fifty of the best of our people and put them under the command of Tamas, my son, and sent them to ambush the pass, for against the Matabele warriors on the plain we, who are not warlike, do not dare to fight.

"The Black One went with them, and when he saw how sore was your strait, wished to run down to meet the Matabele, for he is a brave man. But I had said to Tamas—'No, do not try to fight them in the open, for there they will certainly kill you.' Moreover, Lady, I was sure that you would reach the top of the poort. Well, you reached it, though but by the breadth of a blade of grass, and my children shot with the new rifles, and the place being narrow so that they could not miss, killed many of those hyenas of Amandabele. But to kill Matabele is like catching fleas on a dog's back: there are always more. Still it served its turn, you and your father were brought away safely, and we lost no one."

"Where, then, are the Matabele now?" asked Benita.

"Outside our walls, a whole regiment of them: three thousand men or more, under the command of the Captain Maduna, he of the royal blood, whose life you begged, but who nevertheless hunted you like a buck."

"Perhaps he did not know who it was," suggested Benita.

"Perhaps not," the Molimo answered, rubbing his chin, "for in such matters even a Matabele generally keeps faith, and you may remember he promised you life for life. However, they are here ravening like lions round the walls, and that is why we carried you up to the top of the hill, that you might be safe from them."

"But are you safe, my Father?"

"I think so," he replied with a dry little chuckle in his throat. "Whoever built this fortress built it strong, and we have blocked the gates. Also, they caught no one outside; all are within the walls, together with the sheep and goats. Lastly, we have sent most of the women and children across the Zambesi in canoes, to hide in places we know of whither the Amandabele cannot follow, for they dare not swim a river. Therefore, for those of us that remain we have food for three months, and before then the rains will drive the impi out."

"Why did you not all go across the river, Father?"

"For two reasons, Lady. The first is, that if we once abandoned our stronghold, which we have held from the beginning, Lobengula would take it, and keep it, so that we could never re-enter into our heritage, which would be a shame to us and bring down the vengeance of the spirits of our ancestors upon our heads. The second is, that as you have returned to us we stay to protect you."

"You are very good to me," murmured Benita.

"Nay, nay, we brought you here, and we do what I am told to do from Above. Trouble may still come upon you; yes, I think that it will come, but once more I pray you, have no fear, for out of this evil root shall spring a flower of joy," and he rose to go.

"Stay," said Benita. "Has the chief Meyer found the gold?"

"No; he has found nothing; but he hunts and hunts like a hungry jackal digging for a bone. But that bone is not for him; it is for you, Lady, you and you only. Oh! I know, you do not seek, still you shall find. Only the next time that you want help, do not run away into the wilderness. Hear the word of Munwali given by his mouth, the Molimo of Bambatse!" And as he spoke, the old priest backed himself out of the tent, stopping now and again to bow to Benita.

A few minutes later her father entered, looking very weak and shaken, and supporting himself upon a stick. Happy was the greeting of these two who, with their arms about each other's neck, gave thanks for their escape from great peril.

"You see, Benita, we can't get away from this place," Mr. Clifford said presently. "We must find that gold."

"Bother the gold," she answered with energy; "I hate its very name. Who can think of gold with three thousand Matabele waiting to kill us?"

"Somehow I don't feel afraid of them any more," said her father; "they have had their chance and lost it, and the Makalanga swear that now they have guns to command the gates, the fortress cannot be stormed. Still, I am afraid of someone."

"Who?"

"Jacob Mayer. I have seen him several times, and I think that he is going mad."

"The Molimo said that too, but why?"

"From the look of him. He sits about muttering and glowing with those dark eyes of his, and sometimes groans, and sometimes bursts into shouts of laughter. That is when the fit is on him, for generally he seems right enough. But get up if you think you can, and you shall judge for yourself."

"I don't want to," said Benita feebly. "Father, I am more afraid of him now than ever. Oh! why did you not let me stop down below, among the Makalanga, instead of carrying me up here again, where we must live alone with that terrible Jew?"

"I wished to, dear, but the Molimo said we should be safer above, and ordered his people to carry you up. Also, Jacob swore that unless you were brought back he would kill me. Now you understand why I believe that he is mad."

"Why, why?" gasped Benita again.

"God knows," he answered with a groan; "but I think that he is sure that we shall never find the gold without you, since the Molimo has told him that it is for you and you alone, and he says the old man has second sight, or something of the sort. Well, he would have murdered me—I saw it in his eye—so I thought it better to give in rather than that you should be left here sick and alone. Of course there was one way——" and he paused.

She looked at him and asked:

"What way?"

"To shoot him before he shot me," he answered in a whisper, "for your sake, dear—but I could not bring myself to do it."

"No," she said with a shudder, "not that—not that. Better that we should die than that his blood should be upon our hands. Now I will get up and try to show no fear. I am sure that is best, and perhaps we shall be able to escape somehow. Meanwhile, let us humour him, and pretend to go on looking for this horrible treasure."

So Benita rose to discover that, save for her stiffness, she was but little the worse, and finding all things placed in readiness, set to work with her father's help to cook the evening meal as usual. Of Meyer, who doubtless had placed things in readiness, she saw nothing.

Before nightfall he came, however, as she knew he would. Indeed, although she heard no step and her back was towards him, she felt his presence; the sense of it fell upon her like a cold shadow. Turning round she beheld the man. He was standing close by, but above her, upon a big granite boulder, in climbing which his soft veld schoons, or hide shoes, had made no noise, for Meyer could move like a cat. The last rays from the sinking sun struck him full, outlining his agile, nervous shape against the sky, and in their intense red light, which flamed upon him, he appeared terrible. He looked like a panther about to spring; his eyes shone like a panther's, and Benita knew that she was the prey whom he desired. Still, remembering her resolution, she determined to show no fear, and addressed him:

"Good-evening, Mr. Meyer. Oh! I am so stiff that I cannot lift my neck to look at you," and she laughed.

He bounded softly from the rock, like a panther again, and stood in front of her.

"You should thank the God you believe in," he said, "that by now you are not stiff indeed—all that the jackals have left of you."

"I do, Mr. Meyer, and I thank you, too; it was brave of you to come out to save us. Father," she called, "come and tell Mr. Meyer how grateful we are to him."

Mr. Clifford hobbled out from his hut under the tree, saying:

"I have told him already, dear."

"Yes," answered Jacob, "you have told me; why repeat yourself? I see that supper is ready. Let us eat, for you must be hungry; afterwards I have something to tell you."

So they ate, with no great appetite, any of them—indeed Meyer touched but little food, though he drank a good deal, first of strong black coffee and afterwards of squareface and water. But on Benita he pressed the choicest morsels that he could find, eyeing her all the while, and saying that she must take plenty of nutriment or her beauty would suffer and her strength wane. Benita bethought her of the fairy tales of her childhood, in which the ogre fed up the princess whom he purposed to devour.

"You should think of your own strength, Mr. Meyer," she said; "you cannot live on coffee and squareface."

"It is all I need to-night. I am astonishingly well since you came back. I can never remember feeling so well, or so strong. I can do the work of three men, and not be tired; all this afternoon, for instance, I have been carrying provisions and other things up that steep wall, for we must prepare for a long siege together; yet I should never know that I had lifted a single basket. But while you were away—ah! then I felt tired."

Benita changed the subject, asking him if he had made any discoveries.

"Not yet, but now that you are back the discoveries will soon come. Do not be afraid; I have my plan which cannot fail. Also, it was lonely working in that cave without you, so I only looked about a little outside till it was time to go to meet you, and shoot some of those Matabele. Do you know?—I killed seven of them myself. When I was shooting for your sake I could not miss," and he smiled at her.

Benita shrank from him visibly, and Mr. Clifford said in an angry voice:

"Don't talk of those horrors before my daughter. It is bad enough to have to do such things, without speaking about them afterwards."

"You are right," he replied reflectively; "and I apologise, though personally I never enjoyed anything so much as shooting those Matabele. Well, they are gone, and there are plenty more outside. Listen! They are singing their evening hymn," and with his long finger he beat time to the volleying notes of the dreadful Matabele war-chant, which floated up from the plain below. "It sounds quite religious, doesn't it? only the words—no, I will not translate them. In our circumstances they are too personal.

"Now I have something to say to you. It was unkind of you to run away and leave me like that, not honourable either. Indeed," he added with a sudden outbreak of the panther ferocity, "had you alone been concerned, Clifford, I tell you frankly that when we met again, I should have shot you. Traitors deserve to be shot, don't they?"

"Please stop talking to my father like that," broke in Benita in a stern voice, for her anger had overcome her fear. "Also it is I whom you should blame."

"It is a pleasure to obey you," he answered bowing; "I will never mention the subject any more. Nor do I blame you—who could?—not Jacob Meyer. I quite understand that you found it very dull up here, and ladies must be allowed their fancies. Also you have come back; so why talk of the matter? But listen: on one point I have made up my mind; for your own sake you shall not go away any more until we leave this together. When I had finished carrying up the food I made sure of that. If you go to look to-morrow morning you will find that no one can come up that wall—and, what is more, no one can go down it. Moreover, that I may be quite certain, in future I shall sleep near the stair myself."

Benita and her father stared at each other.

"The Molimo has a right to come," she said; "it is his sanctuary."

"Then he must celebrate his worship down below for a little while. The old fool pretends to know everything, but he never guessed what I was going to do. Besides, we don't want him breaking in upon our privacy, do we? He might see the gold when we find it, and rob us of it afterwards."

XVII.
THE FIRST EXPERIMENT

Again Benita and her father stared at each other blankly, almost with despair. They were trapped, cut off from all help; in the power of a man who was going mad. Mr. Clifford said nothing. He was old and growing feeble; for years, although he did not know it, Meyer had dominated him, and never more so than in this hour of stress and bewilderment. Moreover, the man had threatened to murder him, and he was afraid, not so much for himself as for his daughter. If he were to die now, what would happen to her, left alone with Jacob Meyer? The knowledge of his own folly, understood too late, filled him with shame. How could he have been so wicked as to bring a girl upon such a quest in the company of an unprincipled Jew, of whose past he knew nothing except that it was murky and dubious? He had committed a great crime, led on by a love of lucre, and the weight of it pressed upon his tongue and closed his lips; he knew not what to say.

For a little while Benita was silent also; hope died within her. But she was a bold-spirited woman, and by degrees her courage re-asserted itself. Indignation filled her breast and shone through her dark eyes. Suddenly she turned upon Jacob, who sat before them smoking his pipe and enjoying their discomfiture.

"How dare you?" she asked in a low, concentrated voice. "How dare you, you coward?"

He shrank a little beneath her scorn and anger; then seemed to recover and brace himself, as one does who feels that a great struggle is at hand, upon the issue of which everything depends.

"Do not be angry with me," he answered. "I cannot bear it. It hurts—ah! you don't know how it hurts. Well, I will tell you, and before your father, for that is more honourable. I dare—for your sake."

"For my sake? How can it benefit me to be cooped up in this horrible place with you? I would rather trust myself with the Makalanga, or even," she added with bitter scorn, "even with those bloody-minded Matabele."

"You ran away from them very fast a little while ago, Miss Clifford. But you do not understand me. When I said for your sake, I meant for my own. See, now. You tried to leave me the other day and did not succeed. Another time you might succeed, and then—what would happen to me?"

"I do not know, Mr. Meyer," and her eyes added—"I do not care."

"Ah! but I know. Last time it drove me nearly mad; next time I should go quite mad."

"Because you believe that through me you will find this treasure of which you dream day and night, Mr. Meyer——"

"Yes," he interrupted quickly. "Because I believe that in you I shall find the treasure of which I dream day and night, and because that treasure has become necessary to my life."

Benita turned quickly towards her father, who was puzzling over the words, but before either of them could speak Jacob passed his hand across his brow in a bewildered way and said:

"What was I talking of? The treasure, yes, the uncountable treasure of pure gold, that lies hid so deep, that is so hard to discover and to possess; the useless, buried treasure that would bring such joy and glory to us both, if only it could be come at and reckoned out, piece by piece, coin by coin, through the long, long years of life."

Again he paused; then went on.

"Well, Miss Clifford, you are quite right; that is why I have dared to make you a prisoner, because, as the old Molimo said, the treasure is yours and I wish to share it. Now, about this treasure, it seems that it can't be found, can it, although I have worked so hard?" and he looked at his delicate, scarred hands.

"Quite so, Mr. Meyer, it can't be found, so you had better let us go down to the Makalanga."

"But there is a way, Miss Clifford, there is a way. You know where it lies, and you can show me."

"If I knew I would show you soon enough, Mr. Meyer, for then you could take the stuff and our partnership would be at an end."

"Not until it is divided ounce by ounce and coin by coin. But first—first you must show me, as you say you will, and as you can."

"How, Mr. Meyer? I am not a magician."

"Ah! but you are. I will tell you how, having your promise. Listen now, both of you. I have studied. I know a great many secret things, and I read in your face that you have the gift—let me look in your eyes a while, Miss Clifford, and you will go to sleep quite gently, and then in your sleep, which shall not harm you at all, you will see where that gold lies hidden, and you will tell us."

"What do you mean?" asked Benita, bewildered.

"I know what he means," broke in Mr. Clifford. "You mean that you want to mesmerize her as you did the Zulu chief."

Benita opened her lips to speak, but Meyer said quickly:

"No, no; hear me first before you refuse. You have the gift, the precious gift of clairvoyance, that is so rare."

"How do you know that, Mr. Meyer? I have never been mesmerized in my life."

"It does not matter how. I do know it; I have been sure of it from the moment when first we met, that night by the kloof. Although, perhaps, you felt nothing then, it was that gift of yours working upon a mind in tune, my mind, which led me there in time to save you, as it was that gift of yours which warned you of the disaster about to happen to the ship—oh! I have heard the story from your own lips. Your spirit can loose itself from the body: it can see the past and the future; it can discover the hidden things."

"I do not believe it," answered Benita; "but at least it shall not be loosed by you."

"It shall, it shall," he cried with passion, his eyes blazing on her as he spoke. "Oh! I foresaw all this, and that is why I was determined you should come with us, so that, should other means fail, we might have your power to fall back upon. Well, they have failed; I have been patient, I have said nothing, but now there is no other way. Will you be so selfish, so cruel, as to deny me, you who can make us all rich in an hour, and take no hurt at all, no more than if you had slept awhile?"

"Yes," answered Benita. "I refuse to deliver my will into the keeping of any living man, and least of all into yours, Mr. Meyer."

He turned to her father with a gesture of despair.

"Cannot you persuade her, Clifford? She is your daughter, she will obey you."

"Not in that," said Benita.

"No," answered Mr. Clifford. "I cannot, and I wouldn't if I could. My daughter is quite right. Moreover, I hate this supernatural kind of thing. If we can't find this gold without it, then we must let it alone, that is all."

Meyer turned aside to hide his face, and presently looked up again, and spoke quite softly.

"I suppose that I must accept my answer, but when you talked of any living man just now, Miss Clifford, did you include your father?"

She shook her head.

"Then will you allow him to try to mesmerize you?"

Benita laughed.

"Oh, yes, if he likes," she said. "But I do not think that the operation will be very successful."

"Good, we will see to-morrow. Now, like you, I am tired. I am going to bed in my new camp by the wall," he added significantly.

"Why are you so dead set against this business?" asked her father, when he had gone.

"Oh, father!" she answered, "can't you see, don't you understand? Then it is hard to have to tell you, but I must. In the beginning Mr. Meyer only wanted the gold. Now he wants more, me as well as the gold. I hate him! You know that is why I ran away. But I have read a good deal about this mesmerism, and seen it once or twice, and who knows? If once I allow his mind to master my mind, although I hate him so much, I might become his slave."

"I understand now," said Mr. Clifford. "Oh, why did I ever bring you here? It would have been better if I had never seen your face again."

On the morrow the experiment was made. Mr. Clifford attempted to mesmerize his daughter. All the morning Jacob, who, it now appeared, had practical knowledge of this doubtful art, tried to instruct him therein. In the course of the lesson he informed him that for a short period in the past, having great natural powers in that direction, he had made use of them professionally, only giving up the business because he found it wrecked his health. Mr. Clifford remarked that he had never told him that before.

"There are lots of things in my life that I have never told you," replied Jacob with a little secret smile. "For instance, once I mesmerized you, although you did not know it, and that is why you always have to do what I want you to, except when your daughter is near you, for her influence is stronger than mine."

Mr. Clifford stared at him.

"No wonder Benita won't let you mesmerize her," he said shortly.

Then Jacob saw his mistake.

"You are more foolish than I thought," he said. "How could I mesmerize you without your knowing it? I was only laughing at you."

"I didn't see the laugh," replied Mr. Clifford uneasily, and they went on with the lesson.

That afternoon it was put to proof—in the cave itself, where Meyer seemed to think that the influences would be propitious. Benita, who found some amusement in the performance, was seated upon the stone steps underneath the crucifix, one lamp on the altar and others one each side of her.

In front stood her father, staring at her and waving his hands mysteriously in obedience to Jacob's directions. So ridiculous did he look indeed while thus engaged that Benita had the greatest difficulty in preventing herself from bursting into laughter. This was the only effect which his grimaces and gesticulations produced upon her, although outwardly she kept a solemn appearance, and even from time to time shut her eyes to encourage him. Once, when she opened them again, it was to perceive that he was becoming very hot and exhausted, and that Jacob was watching him with such an unpleasant intentness that she re-closed her eyes that she might not see his face.

It was shortly after this that of a sudden Benita did feel something, a kind of penetrating power flowing upon her, something soft and subtle that seemed to creep into her brain like the sound of her mother's lullaby in the dim years ago. She began to think that she was a lost traveller among alpine snows wrapped round by snow, falling, falling in ten myriad flakes, every one of them with a little heart of fire. Then it came to her that she had heard this snow-sleep was dangerous, the last of all sleeps, and that its victims must rouse themselves, or die.

Benita roused herself just in time—only just, for now she was being borne over the edge of a precipice upon the wings of swans, and beneath her was darkness wherein dim figures walked with lamps where their hearts should be. Oh, how heavy were her eyelids! Surely a weight hung to each of them, a golden weight. There, there, they were open, and she saw. Her father had ceased his efforts; he was rubbing his brow with a red pocket-handkerchief, but behind him, with rigid arms outstretched, his glowing eyes fastened on her face, stood Jacob Meyer. By an effort she sprang to her feet, shaking her head as a dog does.

"Have done with this nonsense," she said. "It tires me," and snatching one of the lamps she ran swiftly down the place.

Benita expected that Jacob Meyer would be very angry with her, and braced herself for a scene. But nothing of the sort happened. A while afterwards she saw the two of them approaching, engaged apparently in amicable talk.

"Mr. Meyer says that I am no mesmerist, love," said her father, "and I can quite believe him. But for all that it is a weary job. I am as tired as I was after our escape from the Matabele."

She laughed and answered:

"To judge by results I agree with you. The occult is not in your line, father. You had better give it up."

"Did you, then, feel nothing?" asked Meyer.

"Nothing at all," she answered, looking him in the eyes. "No, that's wrong, I felt extremely bored and sorry to see my father making himself ridiculous. Grey hairs and nonsense of that sort don't go well together."

"No," he answered. "I agree with you—not of that sort," and the subject dropped.

For the next few days, to her intense relief, Benita heard no more of mesmerism. To begin with, there was something else to occupy their minds. The Matabele, tired of marching round the fortress and singing endless war-songs, had determined upon an assault. From their point of vantage on the topmost wall the three could watch the preparations which they made. Trees were cut down and brought in from a great distance that rude ladders might be fashioned out of them; also spies wandered round reconnoitring for a weak place in the defences. When they came too near the Makalanga fired on them, killing some, so that they retreated to the camp, which they had made in a fold of ground at a little distance. Suddenly it occurred to Meyer that although here the Matabele were safe from the Makalanga bullets, it was commanded from the greater eminence, and by way of recreation he set himself to harass them. His rifle was a sporting Martini, and he had an ample supply of ammunition. Moreover, he was a beautiful marksman, with sight like that of a hawk.

A few trial shots gave him the range; it was a shade under seven hundred yards, and then he began operations. Lying on the top of the wall and resting his rifle upon a stone, he waited until the man who was superintending the manufacture of the ladders came out into the open, when, aiming carefully, he fired. The soldier, a white-bearded savage, sprang into the air, and fell backwards, while his companions stared upwards, wondering whence the bullet had come.

"Pretty, wasn't it?" said Meyer to Benita, who was watching through a pair of field-glasses.

"I dare say," she answered. "But I don't want to see any more," and giving the glasses to her father, she climbed down the wall.

But Meyer stayed there, and from time to time she heard the report of his rifle. In the evening he told her that he had killed six men and wounded ten more, adding that it was the best day's shooting which he could remember.

"What is the use when there are so many?" she asked.

"Not much," he answered. "But it annoys them and amuses me. Also, it was part of our bargain that we should help the Makalanga if they were attacked."

"I believe that you like killing people," she said.

"I don't mind it, Miss Clifford, especially as they tried to kill you."

XVIII.
THE OTHER BENITA

At irregular times, when he had nothing else to do, Jacob went on with his man-shooting, in which Mr. Clifford joined him, though with less effect. Soon it became evident that the Matabele were very much annoyed by the fatal accuracy of this fire. Loss of life they did not mind in the abstract, but when none of them knew but that their own turn might come next to perish beneath these downward plunging bullets, the matter wore a different face to them. To leave their camp was not easy, since they had made a thorn *boma* round it, to protect them in case the Makalanga should make a night sally; also they could find no other convenient spot. The upshot of it all was to hurry their assault, which they delivered before they had prepared sufficient ladders to make it effective.

At the first break of dawn on the third day after Mr. Clifford's attempt at mesmerism, Benita was awakened by the sounds of shouts and firing. Having dressed herself hastily, she hurried in the growing light towards that part of the wall from below which the noise seemed to come, and climbing it, found her father and Jacob already seated there, their rifles in hand.

"The fools are attacking the small gate through which you went out riding, Miss Clifford, the very worst place that they could have chosen, although the wall looks very weak there," said the latter. "If those Makalanga have any pluck they ought to teach them a lesson."

Then the sun rose and they saw companies of Matabele, who carried ladders in their hands, rushing onwards through the morning mist till their sight of them was obstructed by the swell of the hill. On these companies the two white men opened fire, with what result they could not see in that light. Presently a great shout announced that the enemy had gained the fosse and were setting up the ladders. Up to this time the Makalanga appeared to have done nothing, but now they began to fire rapidly from the ancient bastions which commanded the entrance the impi was striving to storm, and soon through the thinning fog they perceived wounded Matabele staggering and crawling back towards their camp. Of these, the light now better, Jacob did not neglect to take his toll.

Meanwhile, the ancient fortress rang with the hideous tumult of the attack. It was evident that again and again, as their fierce war-shouts proclaimed, the Matabele were striving to scale the wall, and again and again were beaten back by the raking rifle fire. Once a triumphant yell seemed to announce their success. The fire slackened and Benita grew pale with fear.

"The Makalanga cowards are bolting," muttered Mr. Clifford, listening with terrible anxiety.

But if so their courage came back to them, for presently the guns cracked louder and more incessant than before, and the savage cries of "Kill! Kill! Kill!" dwindled and died away. Another five minutes and the Matabele were in full retreat, bearing with them many dead and wounded men upon their backs or stretched out on the ladders.

"Our Makalanga friends should be grateful to us for those hundred rifles," said Jacob as he loaded and fired rapidly, sending his bullets wherever the clusters were thickest. "Had it not been for them their throats would have been cut by now," he added, "for they could never have stopped those savages with the spear."

"Yes, and ours too before nightfall," said Benita with a shudder, for the sight of this desperate fray and fear of how it might end had sickened her. "Thank Heaven, it is over! Perhaps they will give up the siege and go away."

But, notwithstanding their costly defeat, for they had lost over a hundred men, the Matabele, who were afraid to return to Buluwayo except as victors, did nothing of the sort. They only cut down a quantity of reeds and scrub, and moved their camp nearly to the banks of the river, placing it in such a position that it could no longer be searched by the fire of the two white men. Here they sat themselves down sullenly, hoping to starve out the garrison or to find some other way of entering the fortress.

Now Meyer's shooting having come to an end for lack of men to shoot at, since the enemy exposed themselves no more, he was again able to give his full attention to the matter of the treasure hunt.

As nothing could be found in the cave he devoted himself to the outside enclosure which, it may be remembered, was grown over with grass and trees and crowded with ruins. In the most important of these ruins they began to dig somewhat aimlessly, and were rewarded by finding a certain amount of gold in the shape of beads and ornaments, and a few more skeletons of ancients. But of the Portuguese hoard there was no sign. Thus it came about that they grew gloomier day by day, till at last they scarcely spoke to each other. Jacob's angry disappointment was written on his face, and Benita was filled with despair, since to escape from their gaoler above and the Matabele below seemed impossible. Moreover, she had another cause for anxiety.

The ill-health which had been threatening her father for a long while now fell upon him in earnest, so that of a sudden he became a very old man. His strength and energy left him, and his mind was so filled with remorse for what he held to be his crime in bringing his daughter to this awful place, and with terror for the fate that threatened her, that he could think of nothing else. In vain did she try to comfort him. He would only wring his hands and groan, praying that God and she would forgive him. Now, too, Meyer's mastery over him became continually more evident. Mr. Clifford implored the man, almost with tears, to unblock the wall and allow them to go down to the Makalanga. He even tried to bribe him with the offer of all his share of the treasure, if it were found, and when that failed, of his property in the Transvaal.

But Jacob only told him roughly not to be a fool, as they had to see the thing through together. Then he would go again and brood by himself, and Benita noticed that he always took his rifle or a pistol with him. Evidently he feared lest her father should catch him unprepared, and take the law into his own hands by means of a sudden bullet.

One comfort she had, however: although he watched her closely, the Jew never tried to molest her in any way, not even with more of his enigmatic and amorous speeches. By degrees, indeed, she came to believe that all this was gone from his mind, or that he had abandoned his advances as hopeless.

A week passed since the Matabele attack, and nothing had happened. The Makalanga took no notice of them, and so far as she was aware the old Molimo never attempted to climb the blocked wall or otherwise to communicate with them, a thing so strange that, knowing his affection for her, Benita came to the conclusion that he must be dead, killed perhaps in the attack. Even Jacob Meyer had abandoned his digging, and sat about all day doing nothing but think.

Their meal that night was a miserable affair, since in the first place provisions were running short and there was little to eat, and in the second no one spoke a word. Benita could swallow no food; she was weary of that sun-dried trek-ox, for since Meyer had blocked the wall they had little else. But by good fortune there remained plenty of coffee, and of this she drank two cups, which Jacob prepared and handed to her with much politeness. It tasted very bitter to her, but this, Benita reflected, was because they lacked milk and sugar. Supper ended, Meyer rose and bowed to her, muttering that he was going to bed, and a few minutes later Mr. Clifford followed his example. She went with her father to the hut beneath the tree, and having helped him to remove his coat, which now he seemed to find difficulty in doing for himself, bade him good-night and returned to the fire.

It was very lonely there in the silence, for no sound came from either the Matabele or the Makalanga camps, and the bright moonlight seemed to people the place with fantastic shadows that looked alive. Benita cried a little now that her father could not see her, and then also sought refuge in bed. Evidently the end, whatever it might be, was near, and of it she could not bear to think. Moreover, her eyes were strangely heavy, so much so that before she had finished saying her prayers sleep fell upon her, and she knew no more.

Had she remained as wakeful as it was often her fate to be during those fearful days, towards midnight she might have heard some light-footed creature creeping to her tent, and seen that the moon-rays which flowed through the gaping and ill-closed flap were cut off by the figure of a man with glowing eyes, whose projected arms waved over her mysteriously. But Benita neither heard nor saw. In her drugged rest she did not know that her sleep turned gradually to a magic swoon. She had no knowledge of her rising, or of how she threw her thick cloak about her, lit her lamp, and, in obedience to that beckoning finger, glided from the tent. She never heard her father stumble from his hut, disturbed by the sound of footsteps, or the words that passed between him and Jacob Meyer, while, lamp in hand, she stood near them like a strengthless ghost.

"If you dare to wake her," hissed Jacob, "I tell you that she will die, and afterwards you shall die," and he fingered the pistol at his belt. "No harm shall come to her—I swear it! Follow and see. Man, man, be silent; our fortunes hang on it."

Then, overcome also by the strange fierceness of that voice and gaze, he followed.

On they go to the winding neck of the cavern, first Jacob walking backwards like the herald of majesty; then majesty itself in the shape of this long-haired, death-like woman, cloaked and bearing in her hand the light; and last, behind, the old, white-bearded man, like Time following Beauty to the grave. Now they were in the great cavern, and now, avoiding the open tombs, the well mouth and the altar, they stood beneath the crucifix.

"Be seated," said Meyer, and the entranced Benita sat herself down upon the steps at the foot of the cross, placing the lamp on the rock pavement before her, and bowing her head till her hair fell upon her naked feet and hid them. He held his hands above her for a while, then asked:

"Do you sleep?"

"I sleep," came the strange, slow answer.

"Is your spirit awake?"

"It is awake."

"Command it to travel backwards through the ages to the beginning, and tell me what you see here."

"I see a rugged cave and wild folk dwelling in it; an old man is dying yonder," and she pointed to the right; "and a black woman with a babe at her breast tends him. A man, it is her husband, enters the cave. He holds a torch in one hand, and with the other drags a buck."

"Cease," said Meyer. "How long is this ago?"

"Thirty-three thousand two hundred and one years," came the answer, spoken without any hesitation.

"Pass on," he said, "pass on thirty thousand years, and tell me what you see."

For a long while there was silence.

"Why do you not speak?" he asked.

"Be patient; I am living through those thirty thousand years; many a life, many an age, but none may be missed."

Again there was silence for a long while, till at length she spoke:

"They are done, all of them, and now three thousand years ago I see this place changed and smoothly fashioned, peopled by a throng of worshippers clad in strange garments with clasps upon them. Behind me stands the graven statue of a goddess with a calm and cruel face, in front of the altar burns a fire, and on the altar white-robed priests are sacrificing an infant which cries aloud."

"Pass on, pass on," Meyer said hurriedly, as though the horror of that scene had leapt to his eyes. "Pass on two thousand seven hundred years and tell me what you see."

Again there was a pause, while the spirit he had evoked in the body of Benita lived through those ages. Then slowly she answered:

"Nothing, the place is black and desolate, only the dead sleep beneath its floor."

"Wait till the living come again," he commanded; "then speak."

"They are here," she replied presently. "Tonsured monks, one of whom fashions this crucifix, and their followers who bow before the Host upon the altar. They come, they go—of whom shall I tell you?"

"Tell me of the Portuguese; of those who were driven here to die."

"I see them all," she answered, after a pause. "Two hundred and three of them. They are ragged and wayworn and hungry. Among them is a beautiful woman, a girl. She draws near to me, she enters into me. You must ask her,"—this was spoken in a very faint voice—"I am I no more."

Mr. Clifford attempted to interrupt, but fiercely Meyer bade him to be silent.

"Speak," he commanded, but the crouching figure shook her head.

"Speak," he said again, whereon another voice, not that of Benita, answered in another tongue:

"I hear; but I do not understand your language."

"Great Heaven!" said Meyer, "it is Portuguese," and for a while the terror of the thing struck him dumb, for he was aware that Benita knew no Portuguese. He knew it, however, who had lived at Lorenço Marquez.

"Who are you?" he asked in that tongue.

"I am Benita da Ferreira. I am the daughter of the Captain da Ferreira and of his wife, the lady Christinha, who stand by you now. Turn, and you will see them."

Jacob started and looked about him uneasily.

"What did she say? I did not catch it all," asked Mr. Clifford.

He translated her words.

"But this is black magic," exclaimed the old man. "Benita knows no Portuguese, so how comes she to speak it?"

"Because she is no longer our Benita; she is another Benita, Benita da Ferreira. The Molimo was right when he said that the spirit of the dead woman went with her, as it seems the name has gone," he added.

"Have done," said Mr. Clifford; "the thing is unholy. Wake her up, or I will."

"And bring about her death. Touch or disturb her, and I tell you she will die," and he pointed to Benita, who crouched before them so white and motionless that indeed it seemed as though already she were dead. "Be quiet," he went on. "I swear to you that no hurt shall come to her, also that I will translate everything to you. Promise, or I will tell you nothing, and her blood be on your head."

Then Mr. Clifford groaned and said:

"I promise."

"Tell me your story, Benita da Ferreira. How came you and your people here?"

"The tribes of Monomotapa rose against our rule. They killed many of us in the lower land, yes, they killed my brother and him to whom I was affianced. The rest of us fled north to this ancient fortress, hoping thence to escape by the river, the Zambesi. The Mambo, our vassal, gave us shelter here, but the tribes besieged the walls in thousands, and burnt all the boats so that we could not fly by the water. Many times we beat them back from the wall; the ditch was full of their dead, and at last they dared to attack no more.

"Then we began to starve and they won the first wall. We went on starving and they won the second wall, but the third wall they could not climb. So we died; one by one we laid ourselves down in this cave and died, till I alone was left, for while our people had food they gave it to me who was the daughter of their captain. Yes, alone I knelt at the foot of this crucifix by the body of my father, praying to the blessed Son of Mary for the death that would not come, and kneeling there I swooned. When I awoke again the Mambo and his men stood about me, for now, knowing us to be dead, the tribes had gone, and those who were in hiding across the river had returned and knew how to climb the wall. They bore me from among the dead, they gave me food so that my strength came back; but in the night I, who in my wickedness would not live, escaped from them and climbed the pillar of black rock, so that when the sun rose they saw me standing there. They begged of me to come down, promising to protect me, but I said 'No,' who in the evil of my heart only desired to die, that I might join my father and my brother, and one who was dearer to me than all. They asked of me where the great treasure was hidden."

At these words Jacob gasped, then rapidly translated them, while the figure before them became silent, as though it felt that for the moment the power of his will was withdrawn.

"Speak on, I bid you," he said, and she continued, the rich, slow voice dropping word after word from the lips of Benita in the alien speech that this Benita never knew.

"I answered that it was where it was, and that if they gave it up to any save the one appointed, then that fate which had befallen my people would befall theirs also. Yes, I gave it into their keeping until I came again, since with his dying breath my father had commanded me to reveal it to none, and I believed that I who was about to die should never come again.

"Then I made my last prayer, I kissed the golden crucifix that now hangs upon this breast wherein I dwell," and the hand of the living Benita was lifted, and moving like the hand of a dead thing, slowly drew out the symbol from beneath the cloak, held it for a moment in the lamplight, and let it fall to its place again. "I put my hands before my eyes that I might not see, and I hurled myself from the pinnacle."

Now the voice ceased, but from the lips came a dreadful sound, such as might be uttered by one whose bones are shattered upon rocks, followed by other sounds like those of one who chokes in water. They were so horrible to hear that Mr. Clifford nearly fainted, and even Jacob Meyer staggered and turned white as the white face of Benita.

"Wake her! For God's sake, wake her!" said her father. "She is dying, as that woman died hundreds of years ago."

"Not till she has told us where the gold is. Be quiet, you fool. She does not feel or suffer. It is the spirit within her that lives through the past again."

Once more there was silence. It seemed as though the story were all told and the teller had departed.

"Benita da Ferreira," said Meyer at length, "I command you, tell me, are you dead?"

"Oh! would that I were dead, as my body is dead!" wailed the lips of Benita. "Alas! I cannot die who suffer this purgatory, and must dwell on here alone until the destined day. Yes, yes, the spirit of her who was Benita da Ferreira must haunt this place in solitude. This is her doom, to be the guardian of that accursed gold which was wrung from the earth by cruelty and paid for with the lives of men."

"Is it still safe?" whispered Jacob.

"I will look;" then after a pause, "I have looked. It is there, every grain of it, in ox-hide bags; only one of them has fallen and burst, that which is black and red."

"Where is it?" he said again.

"I may not tell you; never, never."

"Is there anyone whom you may tell?"

"Yes."

"Whom?"

"Her in whose breast I lie."

"Tell her then."

"I have told her; she knows."

"And may she tell me?"

"Let her guard the secret as she will. O my Guardian, I thank thee. My burden is departed; my sin of self-murder is atoned."

"Benita da Ferreira, are you gone?"

No answer.

"Benita Clifford, do you hear me?"

"I hear you," said the voice of Benita, speaking in English, although Jacob, forgetting, had addressed her in Portuguese.

"Where is the gold?"

"In my keeping."

"Tell me, I command you."

But no words came; though he questioned her many times no words came, till at last her head sank forward upon her knees, and in a faint voice she murmured:

"Loose me, or I die."

XIX.
THE AWAKING

Still Jacob Meyer hesitated. The great secret was unlearned, and, if this occasion passed, might never be learned. But if he hesitated, Mr. Clifford did not. The knowledge of his child's danger, the sense that her life was mysteriously slipping away from her under pressure of the ghastly spell in which she lay enthralled, stirred him to madness. His strength and manhood came back to him. He sprang straight at Meyer's throat, gripped it with one hand, and with the other drew the knife he wore.

"You devil!" he gasped. "Wake her or you shall go with her!" and he lifted the knife.

Then Jacob gave in. Shaking off his assailant he stepped to Benita, and while her father stood behind him with the lifted blade, began to make strange upward passes over her, and to mutter words of command. For a long while they took no effect; indeed, both of them were almost sure that she was gone. Despair gripped her father, and Meyer worked at his black art so furiously that the sweat burst out upon his forehead and fell in great drops to the floor.

Oh, at last, at last she stirred! Her head lifted itself a little, her breast heaved.

"Lord in Heaven, I have saved her!" muttered Jacob in German, and worked on.

Now the eyes of Benita opened, and now she stood up and sighed. But she said nothing; only like a person walking in her sleep, she began to move towards the entrance of the cave, her father going before her with the lamp. On she went, and out of it straight to her tent, where instantly she cast herself upon her bed and sank into deep slumber. It was as though the power of the drug-induced oblivion, which for a while was over-mastered by that other stronger power invoked by Jacob, had reasserted itself.

Meyer watched her for awhile; then said to Mr. Clifford:

"Don't be afraid and don't attempt to disturb her. She will wake naturally in the morning."

"I hope so for both our sakes," he answered, glaring at him, "for if not, you or I, or the two of us, will never see another."

Meyer took no notice of his threats; indeed the man seemed so exhausted that he could scarcely stand.

"I am done," he said. "Now, as she is safe, I don't care what happens to me. I must rest," and he staggered from the tent, like a drunken man.

Outside, at the place where they ate, Mr. Clifford heard him gulping down raw gin from the bottle. Then he heard no more.

All the rest of the night, and for some hours of the early morning, did her father watch by the bed of Benita, although, lightly clad as he was, the cold of dawn struck to his bones. At length, when the sun was well up, she rose in her bed, and her eyes opened.

"What are you doing here, father?" she said.

"I have come to see where you were, dear. You are generally out by now."

"I suppose that I must have overslept myself then," she replied wearily. "But it does not seem to have refreshed me much, and my head aches. Oh! I remember," she added with a start. "I have had such a horrid dream."

"What about?" he asked as carelessly as he could.

"I can't recall it quite, but it had to do with Mr. Meyer," and she shivered. "It seemed as though I had passed into his power, as though he had taken possession of me, body and soul, and forced me to tell him all the secret things."

"What secret things, Benita?"

She shook her head.

"I don't know now, but we went away among dead people, and I told him there. Oh! father, I am afraid of that man—terribly afraid! Protect me from him," and she began to cry a little.

"Of course I will protect you, dear. Something has upset your nerves. Come, dress yourself and you'll soon forget it all. I'll light the fire."

A quarter of an hour later Benita joined him, looking pale and shaken, but otherwise much as usual. She was ravenously hungry, and ate of the biscuits and dried meat with eagerness.

"The coffee tastes quite different from that which I drank last night," she said. "I think there must have been something in it which gave me those bad dreams. Where is Mr. Meyer? Oh, I know!" and again she put her hand to her head. "He is still asleep by the wall."

"Who told you that?"

"I can't say, but it is so. He will not come here till one o'clock. There, I feel much better now. What shall we do, father?"

"Sit in the sun and rest, I think, dear."

"Yes, let us do that, on the top of the wall. We can see the Makalanga from there, and it will be a comfort to be sure that there are other human beings left in the world besides ourselves and Jacob Meyer."

So presently they went, and from the spot whence Meyer used to shoot at the Matabele camp, looked down upon the Makalanga moving about the first enclosure far below. By the aid of the glasses Benita even thought that she recognised Tamas, although of this it was difficult to be sure, for they were all very much alike. Still, the discovery quite excited her.

"I am sure it is Tamas," she said. "And oh! how I wish that we were down there with him, although it is true that then we should be nearer to the Matabele. But they are better than Mr. Meyer, much better."

Now for a while they were silent, till at length she said suddenly:

"Father, you are keeping something back from me, and things begin to come back. Tell me; did I go anywhere last night with Mr. Meyer—you and he and I together?"

He hesitated and looked guilty; Mr. Clifford was not a good actor.

"I see that we did; I am sure that we did. Father, tell me. I must know, I will know."

Then he gave way.

"I didn't want to speak, dear, but perhaps it is best. It is a very strange story. Will you promise not to be upset?"

"I will promise not to be more upset than I am at present," she answered, with a sad little laugh. "Go on."

"You remember that Jacob Meyer wanted to mesmerize you?"

"I am not likely to forget it," she answered.

"Well, last night he did mesmerize you."

"What?" she said. "*What?* Oh! how dreadful! Now I understand it all. But when?"

"When you were sound asleep, I suppose. At least, the first I knew of it was that some noise woke me, and I came out of the hut to see you following him like a dead woman, with a lamp in your hand."

Then he told her all the story, while she listened aghast.

"How dared he!" she gasped, when her father had finished the long tale. "I hate him; I almost wish that you had killed him," and she clenched her little hands and shook them in the air.

"That is not very Christian of you, Miss Clifford," said a voice behind her. "But it is past one o'clock, and as I am still alive I have come to tell you that it is time for luncheon."

Benita wheeled round upon the stone on which she sat, and there, standing amidst the bushes a little way from the foot of the wall, was Jacob Meyer. Their eyes met; hers were full of defiance, and his of conscious power.

"I do not want any luncheon, Mr. Meyer," she said.

"But I am sure that you do. Please come down and have some. Please come down."

The words were spoken humbly, almost pleadingly, yet to Benita they seemed as a command. At any rate, with slow reluctance she climbed down the shattered wall, followed by her father, and without speaking they went back to their camping place, all three of them, Jacob leading the way.

When they had eaten, or made pretence to eat, he spoke.

"I see that your father has told you everything, Miss Clifford, and of that I am glad. As for me, it would have been awkward, who must ask your forgiveness for so much. But what could I do? I knew, as I have always known, that it was only possible to find this treasure by your help. So I gave you something to make you sleep, and then in your sleep I hypnotized you, and—you know the rest. I have great experience in this art, but I have never seen or heard of anything like what happened, and I hope I never shall again."

Hitherto Benita had sat silent, but now her burning indignation and curiosity overcame her shame and hatred.

"Mr. Meyer," she said, "you have done a shameful and a wicked thing, and I tell you at once that I can never forgive you."

"Don't say that. Please don't say that," he interrupted in tones of real grief. "Make allowances for me. I had to learn, and there was no other way. You are a born clairvoyante, one among ten thousand, my art told me so, and you know all that is at stake."

"By which you mean so many ounces of gold, Mr. Meyer."

"By which I mean the greatness that gold can give, Miss Clifford."

"Such greatness, Mr. Meyer, as a week of fever, or a Matabele spear, or God's will can rob you of. But the thing is done, and soon or late the sin must be paid for. Now I want to ask you a question. You believe in nothing; you have told me so several times. You say that there is no such thing as a spirit, that when we die, we die, and there's an end. Do you not?"

"Yes, I do."

"Then tell me, what was it that spoke out of my lips last night, and how came it that I, who know no Portuguese, talked to you in that tongue?"

He shrugged his shoulders.

"You have put a difficult question, but one I think that can be answered. There is no such thing as a spirit, an identity that survives death. But there is such a thing as the sub-conscious self, which is part of the animating principle of the universe, and, if only its knowledge can be unsealed, knows all that has passed and all that is passing in that universe. One day perhaps you will read the works of my compatriot, Hegel, and there you will find it spoken of."

"You explain nothing."

"I am about to explain, Miss Clifford. Last night I gave to your sub-conscious self—that which knows all—the strength of liberty, so that it saw the past as it happened in this place. Already you knew the story of the dead girl, Benita da Ferreira, and that story you re-enacted, talking the tongue she used as you would have talked Greek or any other tongue, had it been hers. It was not her spirit that animated you, although at the time I called it so for shortness, but your own buried knowledge, tricked out and furnished by the effort of your human imagination. That her name, Benita, should have been yours also is no doubt a strange coincidence, but no more. Also we have no proof that it was so; only what you said in your trance."

"Perhaps," said Benita, who was in no mood for philosophical argument. "Perhaps also one day you will see a spirit, Mr. Meyer, and think otherwise."

"When I see a spirit and know that it is a spirit, then doubtless I shall believe in spirits. But what is the good of talking of such things? I do not seek spirits; I seek Portuguese gold. Now, I am sure you can tell where that gold lies. You would have told us last night, had not your nervous strength failed you, who are unaccustomed to the state of trance. Speaking as Benita da Ferreira, you said that you saw it and described its condition. Then you could, or would, say no more, and it became necessary to waken you. Miss Clifford, you must let me mesmerize you once again for a few minutes only, for then we will waste no time on past histories, and we shall find the gold. Unless, indeed," he added by an afterthought, and looking at her sharply, "you know already where it is; in which case I need not trouble you."

"I do not know, Mr. Meyer. I remember nothing about the gold."

"Which proves my theory. What purported to be the spirit of Benita da Ferreira said that it had passed the secret on to you, but in your waking state you do not know that secret. In fact, she did not pass it on because she had no existence. But in your sub-conscious state you will know. Therefore I must mesmerize you again. Not at once, but in a few days' time, when you have quite recovered. Let us say next Wednesday, three days hence."

"You shall never mesmerize me again, Mr. Meyer."

"No, not while I live," broke in her father, who had been listening to this discussion in silence.

Jacob bowed his head meekly.

"You think so now, but I think otherwise. What I did last night I did against your will, and that I can do again, only much more easily. But I had rather do it with your will, who work not for my own sake only, but for the sake of all of us. And now let us talk no more of the matter, lest we should grow angry." Then he rose and went away.

The next three days were passed by Benita in a state of constant dread. She knew in herself that Jacob Meyer had acquired a certain command over her; that an invincible intimacy had sprung up between them. She was acquainted with his thoughts; thus, before he asked for it, she would find herself passing him some article at table or elsewhere, or answering a question that he was only about to ask. Moreover, he could bring her to him from a little distance. Thus, on two or three occasions when she was wandering about their prison enclosure, as she was wont to do for the sake of exercise, she found her feet draw to some spot—now one place and now another—and when she reached it there before her was Jacob Meyer.

"Forgive me for bringing you here," he would say, smiling after his crooked fashion, and lifting his hat politely, "but I wish to ask you if you have not changed your mind as to being mesmerized?"

Then for a while he would hold her with his eyes, so that her feet seemed rooted to the ground, till at length it was as though he cut a rope by some action of his will and set her free, and, choked with wrath and blind with tears, Benita would turn and run from him as from a wild beast.

But if her days were evil, oh! what were her nights? She lived in constant terror lest he should again drug her food or drink, and, while she slept, throw his magic spell upon her. To protect herself from the first danger she would swallow nothing that had been near him. Now also she slept in the hut with her father, who lay near its door, a loaded rifle at his side, for he had told Jacob outright that if he caught him at his practices he would shoot him, a threat at which the younger man laughed aloud, for he had no fear of Mr. Clifford.

Throughout the long hours of darkness they kept watch alternately, one of them lying down to rest while the other peered and listened. Nor did Benita always listen in vain, for twice at least she heard stealthy footsteps creeping about the hut, and felt that soft and dreadful influence flowing in upon her. Then she would wake her father, whispering, "He is there, I can feel that he is there." But by the time that the old man had painfully dragged himself to his feet—for now he was becoming very feeble and acute rheumatism or some such illness had got hold of him—and crept from the hut, there was no one to be seen. Only through the darkness he would hear the sound of a retreating step, and of low, mocking laughter.

Thus those miserable days went by, and the third morning came, that dreaded Wednesday. Before it was dawn Benita and her father, neither of whom had closed their eyes that night, talked over their strait long and earnestly, and they knew that its crisis was approaching.

"I think that I had better try to kill him, Benita," he said. "I am growing dreadfully weak, and if I put it off I may find no strength, and you will be at his mercy. I can easily shoot him when his back is turned, and though I hate the thought of such a deed, surely I shall be forgiven. Or if not, I cannot help it. I must think of my duty to you, not of myself."

"No, no," she answered. "I will not have it. It would be murder, although he has threatened you. After all, father, I believe that the man is half mad, and not responsible. We must take our chance and trust to God to save us. If He does not," she added, "at the worst I can always save myself," and she touched the pistol which now she wore day and night.

"So be it," said Mr. Clifford, with a groan. "Let us pray for deliverance from this hell and keep our hands clean of blood."

XX.
JACOB MEYER SEES A SPIRIT

For a while they were silent, then Benita said:

"Father, is it not possible that we might escape, after all? Perhaps that stair on the rampart is not so completely blocked that we could not climb over it."

Mr. Clifford, thinking of his stiff limbs and aching back, shook his head and answered:

"I don't know; Meyer has never let me near enough to see."

"Well, why do you not go to look? You know he sleeps till late now, because he is up all night. Take the glasses and examine the top of the wall from inside that old house near by. He will not see or hear you, but if I came near, he would know and wake up."

"If you like, love, I can try, but what are you going to do while I am away?"

"I shall climb the pillar."

"You don't mean — —" and he stopped.

"No, no, nothing of that sort. I shall not follow the example of Benita da Ferreira unless I am driven to it; I want to look, that is all. One can see far from that place, if there is anything to see. Perhaps the Matabele are gone now, we have heard nothing of them lately."

So they dressed themselves, and as soon as the light was sufficiently strong, came out of the hut and parted, Mr. Clifford, rifle in hand, limping off towards the wall, and Benita going towards the great cone. She climbed it easily enough, and stood in the little cup-like depression on its dizzy peak, waiting for the sun to rise and disperse the mists which hung over the river and its banks.

Now whatever may have been the exact ceremonial use to which the ancients put this pinnacle, without doubt it had something to do with sun-worship. This, indeed, was proved by the fact that, at any rate at this season of the year, the first rays of the risen orb struck full upon its point. Thus it came about that, as she stood there waiting, Benita of a sudden found herself suffused in light so vivid and intense that, clothed as she was in a dress which had once been white, it must have caused her to shine like a silver image. For several minutes, indeed, this golden spear of fire blinded her so that she could see nothing, but stood quite still, afraid to move, and waiting until, as the sun grew higher, its level rays passed over her. This they did presently, and plunging into the valley, began to drive away the fog. Now she looked down, along the line of the river.

The Matabele camp was invisible, for it lay in a hollow almost at the foot of the fortress. Beyond it, however, was a rising swell of ground; it may have been half a mile from where she stood, and on the crest of it she perceived what looked like a waggon tent with figures moving round it. They were shouting also, for through the silence of the African morn the sound of their voices floated up to her.

As the mist cleared off Benita saw that without doubt it was a waggon, for there stood the long row of oxen, also it had just been captured by the Matabele, for these were about it in numbers. At the moment, however, they appeared to be otherwise occupied, for they were pointing with their spears to the pillar on Bambatse.

Then it occurred to Benita that, placed as she was in that fierce light with only the sky for background, she must be perfectly visible from the plain below, and that it might be her figure perched like an eagle between heaven and earth which excited their interest. Yes, and not theirs only, for now a white man appeared, who lifted what might have been a gun, or a telescope, towards her. She was sure from the red flannel shirt and the broad hat which he wore that he must be a white man, and oh! how her heart yearned towards him, whoever he might be! The sight of an angel from heaven could scarcely have been more welcome to Benita in her wretchedness.

Yet surely she must be dreaming. What should a white man and a waggon be doing in that place? And why had not the Matabele killed him at once? She could not tell, yet they appeared to have no murderous intentions, since they continued to gesticulate and talk whilst he stared upwards with the telescope, if it were a telescope. So things went on for a long time, for meanwhile the oxen were outspanned, until, indeed, more Matabele arrived, who led off the white man, apparently against his will, towards their camp, where he disappeared. Then there was nothing more to be seen. Benita descended the column.

At its foot she met her father, who had come to seek her.

"What is the matter?" he asked, noting her excited face.

"Oh!" she said or rather sobbed, "there is a waggon with a white man below. I saw the Matabele capture him."

"Then I am sorry for the poor devil," answered the father, "for he is dead by now. But what could a white man have been doing here? Some hunter, I suppose, who has walked into a trap."

The face of Benita fell.

"I hoped," she said, "that he might help us."

"As well might he hope that we could help him. He is gone, and there is an end. Well, peace to his soul, and we have our own troubles to think of. I have been to look at that wall, and it is useless to think of climbing it. If he had been a professional mason, Meyer could not have built it up better; no wonder that we have seen nothing more of the Molimo, for only a bird could reach us."

"Where was Mr. Meyer?" asked Benita.

"Asleep in a blanket under a little shelter of boughs by the stair. At least, I thought so, though it was rather difficult to make him out in the shadow; at any rate, I saw his rifle set against a tree. Come, let us go to breakfast. No doubt he will turn up soon enough."

So they went, and for the first time since the Sunday Benita ate a hearty meal of biscuits soaked in coffee. Although her father was so sure that by now he must have perished on the Matabele spears, the sight of the white man and his waggon had put new life into her, bringing her into touch with the world again. After all, might it not chance that he had escaped?

All this while there had been no sign of Jacob Meyer. This, however, did not surprise them, for now he ate his meals alone, taking his food from a little general store, and cooking it over his own fire. When they had finished their breakfast Mr. Clifford remarked that they had no more drinking water left, and Benita said that she would go to fetch a pailful from the well in the cave. Her father suggested that he should accompany her, but she answered that it was not necessary as she was quite able to wind the chain by herself. So she went, carrying the bucket in one hand and a lamp in the other.

As she walked down the last of the zigzags leading to the cave, Benita stopped a moment thinking that she saw a light, and then went on, since on turning the corner there was nothing but darkness before her. Evidently she had been mistaken. She reached the well and hung the pail on to the great copper hook, wondering as she did so how many folk had done likewise in the far, far past, for the massive metal of that hook was worn quite thin with use. Then she let the roller run, and the sound of the travelling chain clanked dismally in that vaulted, empty place. At length the pail struck the water, and she began to wind up again, pausing at times to rest, for the distance was long and the chain heavy. The bucket appeared. Benita drew it to the side of the well, and lifted it from the hook, then took up her lamp to be gone.

Feeling or seeing something, which she was not sure, she held the lamp above her head, and by its light perceived a figure standing between her and the entrance to the cave.

"Who are you?" she asked, whereon a soft voice answered out of the darkness, the voice of Jacob Meyer.

"Do you mind standing still for a few minutes, Miss Clifford? I have some paper here and I wish to make a sketch. You do not know how beautiful you look with that light above your head illuminating the shadows and the thorn-crowned crucifix beyond. You know, whatever paths fortune may have led me into, by nature I am an artist, and never in my life have I seen such a picture. One day it will make me famous.

'How statue-like I see thee stand!
The agate lamp within thy hand.'

That's what I should put under it; you know the lines, don't you?"

"Yes, Mr. Meyer, but I am afraid you will have to paint your picture from memory, as I cannot hold up this lamp any longer; my arm is aching already. I do not know how you came here, but as you have followed me perhaps you will be so kind as to carry this water."

"I did not follow you, Miss Clifford. Although you never saw me I entered the cave before you to take measurements."

"How can you take measurements in the dark?"

"I was not in the dark. I put out my light when I caught sight of you, knowing that otherwise you would run away, and fate stood me in good stead. You came on, as I willed that you should do. Now let us talk. Miss Clifford, have you changed your mind? You know the time is up."

"I shall never change my mind. Let me pass you, Mr. Meyer."

"No, no, not until you have listened. You are very cruel to me, very cruel indeed. You do not understand that, rather than do you the slightest harm, I would die a hundred times."

"I do not ask you to die; I ask you to leave me alone—a much easier matter."

"But how can I leave you alone when you are a part of me, when—I love you? There, the truth is out, and now say what you will."

Benita lifted the bucket of water; its weight seemed to steady her. Then she put it down again, since escape was impracticable; she must face the situation.

"I have nothing to say, Mr. Meyer, except that I do not love *you* or any living man, and I never shall. I thank you for the compliment you have paid me, and there is an end."

"Any living man," he repeated after her. "That means you love a dead man—Seymour, he who was drowned. No wonder that I hated him when first my eyes fell on him years ago, long before you had come into our lives. Prescience, the sub-conscious self again. Well, what is the use of loving the dead, those who no longer have any existence, who have gone back into the clay out of which they were formed and are not, nor evermore shall be? You have but one life; turn, turn to the living, and make it happy."

"I do not agree with you, Mr. Meyer. To me the dead are still living; one day I shall find them. Now let me go."

"I will not let you go. I will plead and wrestle with you as in the old fable my namesake of my own race wrestled with the angel, until at length you bless me. You despise me because I am a Jew, because I have had many adventures and not succeeded; because you think me mad. But I tell you that there is the seed of greatness in me. Give yourself to me and I will make you great, for now I know that it was you whom I needed to supply what is lacking in my nature. We will win the wealth, and together we will rule——"

"Until a few days hence we starve or the Matabele make an end of us. No, Mr. Meyer, no," and she tried to push past him.

He stretched out his arms and stopped her.

"Listen," he said, "I have pleaded with you as man with woman. Now, as you refuse me and as you alone stand between me and madness, I will take another course. I am your master, your will is servant to my will; I bid you obey me."

He fixed his eyes upon hers, and Benita felt her strength begin to fail.

"Ah!" he said, "you are my servant now, and to show it I shall kiss you on the lips; then I shall throw the sleep upon you, and you will tell me what I want to know. Afterwards we can be wed when it pleases me. Oh! do not think that your father will defend you, for if he interferes I shall kill that foolish old man, whom until now I have only spared for your sake. Remember that if you make me angry, I shall certainly kill him, and your father's blood will be on your head. Now I am going to kiss you."

Benita lifted her hand to find the pistol at her waist. It fell back again; she had no strength; it was as though she were paralysed as a bird is paralysed by a snake so that it cannot open its wings and fly away, but sits there awaiting death. She was given over into the hands of this man whom she hated. Could Heaven allow such a thing? she wondered dimly, and all the while his lips drew nearer to her face.

They touched her own, and then, why or wherefore Benita never understood, the spell broke. All his power was gone, she was as she had been, a free woman, mistress of herself. Contemptuously she thrust the man aside, and, not even troubling to run, lifted her pail of water and walked away.

Soon she saw the light again, and joyfully extinguished her lamp. Indeed, the breast of Benita, which should have been so troubled after the scene through which she had passed, strangely enough was filled with happiness and peace. As that glorious sunlight had broken on her eyes, so had another light of freedom arisen in her soul. She was no longer afraid of Jacob Meyer; that coward kiss of his had struck off the shackles which bound her to him. Her mind had been subject to his mind, but now that his physical nature was brought into the play, his mental part had lost its hold upon her.

As she approached the hut she saw her father seated on a stone outside it, since the poor old man was now so weak and full of pain that he could not stand for very long, and seeing, remembered Meyer's threats against him. At the thought all her new-found happiness departed.

She might be safe; she felt sure that she was safe, but how about her father? If Meyer could not get his way probably he would be as good as his word, and kill him. She shivered at the thought, then, recovering herself, walked forward steadily with her bucket of water.

"You have been a long while gone, my love," said Mr. Clifford.

"Yes, father, Mr. Meyer was in the cave, and kept me."

"How did he get there, and what did he want?"

"I don't know how he got there—crept in when we were not looking, I suppose. But as for what he wanted—listen, dear," and word for word she told him what had passed.

Before she had finished, her father was almost choking with wrath.

"The dirty Jew! The villain!" he gasped. "I never dreamed that he would dare to attempt such an outrage. Well, thank Heaven! I can still hold a rifle, and when he comes out— —"

"Father," she said gently, "that man is mad. He is not responsible for his actions, and therefore, except in self-defence, you must not think of such a thing. As for what he said about you, I believe it was only an empty threat, and for me you need have no fear, his power over me is gone; it went like a flash when his lips touched me," and she rubbed her own as though to wipe away some stain. "I am afraid of nothing more. I believe—yes, I believe the old Molimo was right, and that all will end well— —"

As she was speaking Benita heard a shuffling sound behind her, and turned to learn its cause. Then she saw a strange sight. Jacob Meyer was staggering towards them, dragging one foot after the other through the grass and stones. His face was ghastly pale, his jaw had dropped like that of a dead man, and his eyes were set wide open and full of horror.

"What is the matter with you, man?" asked Mr. Clifford.

"I—I—have seen a ghost," he whispered. "You did not come back into the cave, did you?" he added, pointing at Benita, who shook her head.

"What ghost?" asked Mr. Clifford.

"I don't know, but my lamp went out, and then a light began to shine behind me. I turned, and on the steps of that crucifix I saw a woman kneeling. Her arms clasped the feet of the figure, her forehead rested upon the feet, her long black hair flowed down, she was dressed in white, and the light came from her body and her head. Very slowly she turned and looked at me, and oh, Heaven! that face— —" and he put his hand before his eyes and groaned. "It was beautiful; yes, yes, but fearful to see, like an avenging angel. I fled, and the light—only the light—came with me down the cave, even at the mouth of it there was a little. I have seen a spirit, I who did not believe in spirits, I have seen a spirit, and I tell you that not for all the gold in the world will I enter that place again."

Then before they could answer, suddenly as though his fear had got some fresh hold of him, Jacob sprang forward and fled away, crashing through the bushes and leaping from rock to rock like a frightened buck.

XXI.
THE MESSAGE FROM THE DEAD

"Meyer always said that he did not believe in spirits," remarked Mr. Clifford reflectively.

"Well, he believes in them now," answered Benita with a little laugh. "But, father, the poor man is mad, that is the fact of it, and we must pay no attention to what he says."

"The old Molimo and some of his people—Tamas, for instance— declared that they have seen the ghost of Benita da Ferreira. Are they mad also, Benita?"

"I don't know, father. Who can say? All these things are a mystery. All I do know is that I have never seen a ghost, and I doubt if I ever shall."

"No, but when you were in that trance something that was not you spoke out of your mouth, which something said that it was your namesake, the other Benita. Well, as you say, we can't fathom these things, especially in a haunted kind of place like this, but the upshot of it is that I don't think we have much more to fear from Jacob."

"I am not so sure, father. Mad people change their moods very suddenly."

As it happened Benita was quite right. Towards suppertime Jacob Meyer reappeared, looking pale and shaken, but otherwise much as usual.

"I had a kind of fit this morning," he explained, "the result of an hallucination which seized me when my light went out in that cave. I remember that I thought I had seen a ghost, whereas I know very well that no such thing exists. I was the victim of disappointment, anxieties, and other still stronger emotions," and he looked at Benita. "Therefore, please forget anything I said or did, and—would you give me some supper?"

Benita did so, and he ate in silence, with some heartiness. When he had finished his food, and swallowed two or three tots of squareface, he spoke again:

"I have come here, where I know I am not welcome, upon business," he said in a calm, matter-of-fact voice. "I am tired of this place, and I think it is time that we attained the object of our journey here, namely, to find the hidden gold. That, as we all know, can only be done in a certain way, through the clairvoyant powers of one of us and the hypnotic powers of another. Miss Clifford, I request that you will allow me to throw you into a state of trance. You have told us everything else, but you have not yet told us where the treasure is hidden, and this it is necessary that we should know."

"And if I refuse, Mr. Meyer?"

"Then I am sorry, but I must take means to compel your obedience. Under those circumstances, much against my will, I shall be obliged"—here his eye blazed out wildly—"to execute your father, whose obstinacy and influence stand between us and splendid fortunes. No, Clifford," he added, "don't stretch out your hand towards that rifle, for I am already covering you with the pistol in my pocket, and the moment your hand touches it I shall fire. You poor old man, do you imagine for a single second that, sick as you are, and with your stiff limbs, you can hope to match yourself against my agility, intellect, and strength? Why, I could kill you in a dozen ways before you could lift a finger against me, and by the God I do not believe in, unless your daughter is more compliant, kill you I will!"

"That remains to be seen, my friend," said Mr. Clifford with a laugh, for he was a brave old man. "I am not certain that the God—whom you do not believe in—will not kill you first."

Now Benita, who had been taking counsel with herself, looked up and said suddenly:

"Very well, Mr. Meyer, I consent—because I must. To-morrow morning you shall try to mesmerize me, if you can, in the same place, before the crucifix in the cave."

"No," he answered quickly. "It was not there, it was here, and here it shall be again. The spot you mention is unpropitious to me; the attempt would fail."

"It is the spot that I have chosen," answered Benita stubbornly.

"And this is the spot that I have chosen, Miss Clifford, and my will must prevail over yours."

"Because you who do not believe in spirits are afraid to re-enter the cave, Mr. Meyer, lest you should chance— —"

"Never mind what I am or am not afraid of," he replied with fury. "Make your choice between doing my will and your father's life. To-morrow morning I shall come for your answer, and if you are still obstinate, within half an hour he will be dead, leaving you and me alone together. Oh! you may call me wicked and a villain, but it is you who are wicked, you, you, *you* who force me to this deed of justice."

Then without another word he sprang up and walked away from them backwards, as he went covering Mr. Clifford with the pistol which he had drawn from his pocket. The last that they saw of him were his eyes, which glowered at them through the darkness like those of a lion.

"Father," said Benita, when she was sure that he had gone, "that madman really means to murder you; there is no doubt of it."

"None whatever, dear; if I am alive to-morrow night I shall be lucky, unless I can kill him first or get out of his way."

"Well," she said hurriedly, "I think you can. I have an idea. He is afraid to go into that cave, I am sure. Let us hide ourselves there. We can take food and shall have plenty of water, whereas, unless rain falls, he can get nothing to drink."

"But what then, Benita? We can't stop in the dark for ever."

"No, but we can wait there until something happens. Something must and will happen. His disease won't stand still. He may go raving mad and kill himself. Or he may attempt to attack us, though that is not likely, and then we must do what we can in self defence. Or help may reach us from somewhere. At the worst we shall only die as we should have died outside. Come, let us be quick, lest he should change his mind, and creep back upon us."

So Mr. Clifford gave way, knowing that even if he could steel himself to do the deed of attempting to kill Jacob, he would have little chance against that strong and agile man. Such a struggle would only end in his own death, and Benita must then be left alone with Meyer and his insane passions.

Hurriedly they carried their few belongings into the cave. First they took most of the little store of food that remained, the three hand-lamps and all the paraffin; there was but one tin. Then returning they fetched the bucket, the ammunition, and their clothes. Afterwards, as there was still no sign of Meyer, they even dared to drag in the waggon tent to make a shelter for Benita, and all the wood that they had collected for firing. This proved a wearisome business, for the logs were heavy, and in his crippled state Mr. Clifford could carry no great burden. Indeed, towards the end Benita was forced to complete the task alone, while he limped beside her with his rifle, lest Jacob should surprise them.

When at length everything was done it was long past midnight, and so exhausted were they that, notwithstanding their danger, they flung themselves down upon the canvas tent, which lay in a heap at the end of the cave near the crucifix, and fell asleep.

When Benita woke the lamp had gone out, and it was pitch dark. Fortunately, however, she remembered where she had put the matches and the lantern with a candle in it. She lit the candle and looked at her watch. It was nearly six o'clock. The dawn must be breaking outside, within an hour or two Jacob Meyer would find that they had gone. Suppose that his rage should overcome his fear and that he should creep upon them. They would know nothing of it until his face appeared in the faint ring of light. Or he might even shoot her father out of the darkness. What could she do that would give them warning? A thought came to her.

Taking one of the tent ropes and the lantern, for her father still slept heavily, she went down to the entrance of the cave, and at the end of the last zigzag where once a door had been, managed to make it fast to a stone hinge about eighteen inches above the floor, and on the other side to an eye opposite that was cut in the solid rock to receive a bolt of wood or iron. Meyer, she knew, had no lamps or oil, only matches and perhaps a few candles. Therefore if he tried to enter the cave it was probable that he would trip over the rope and thus give them warning. Then she went back, washed her face and hands with some water that they had drawn on the previous night to satisfy their thirst, and tidied herself as best she could. This done, as her father still slept, she filled the lamps, lit one of them, and looked about her, for she was loth to wake him.

Truly it was an awful place in which to dwell. There above them towered the great white crucifix; there in the corner were piled the remains of the Portuguese. A skull with long hair still hanging to it grinned at her, a withered hand was thrust forward as though to clutch her. Oh, no wonder that in such a spot Jacob Meyer had seen ghosts! In front, too, was the yawning grave where they had found the monk; indeed, his bones wrapped in dark robes still lay within, for Jacob had tumbled them back again. Then beyond and all around deep, dark, and utter silence.

At last her father woke, and glad enough was she of his human company. They breakfasted upon some biscuits and water, and afterwards, while Mr. Clifford watched near the entrance with his rifle, Benita set to work to arrange their belongings. The tent she managed to prop up against the wall of the cave by help of some of the wood which they had carried in. Beneath it she spread their blankets, that it might serve as a sleeping place for them both, and outside placed the food and other things.

While she was thus engaged she heard a sound at the mouth of the cave—Jacob Meyer was entering and had fallen over her rope. Down it she ran, lantern in hand, to her father, who, with his rifle raised, was shouting:

"If you come in here, I put a bullet through you!"

Then came the answer in Jacob's voice, which rang hollow in that vaulted place:

"I do not want to come in; I shall wait for you to come out. You cannot live long in there; the horror of the dark will kill you. I have only to sit in the sunlight and wait."

Then he laughed, and they heard the sound of his footsteps retreating down the passage.

"What are we to do?" asked Mr. Clifford despairingly. "We cannot live without light, and if we have light he will certainly creep to the entrance and shoot us. He is quite mad now; I am sure of it from his voice."

Benita thought a minute, then she answered:

"We must build up the passage. Look," and she pointed to the lumps of rock that the explosion of their mine had shaken down from the roof, and the slabs of cement that they had broken from the floor with the crowbar. "At once, at once," she went on; "he will not come back for some hours, probably not till night."

So they set to work, and never did Benita labour as it was her lot to do that day. Such of the fragments as they could lift they carried between them, others they rolled along by help of the crowbar. For hour after hour they toiled at their task. Luckily for them, the passage was not more than three feet wide by six feet six high, and their material was ample. Before the evening they had blocked it completely with a wall several feet in thickness, which wall they supported on the inside with lengths of the firewood lashed across to the old hinges and bolt-holes, or set obliquely against its face.

It was done, and they regarded their work with pride, although it seemed probable that they were building up their own tomb. Because of its position at an angle of the passage, they knew that Meyer could not get to it with a pole to batter it down. Also, there was no loose powder left, so his only chance would be to pull it to pieces with his hands, and this, they thought, might be beyond his power. At least, should he attempt it, they would have ample warning. Yet that day was not to pass without another trouble.

Just as they had rolled up and levered into place a long fragment of rock designed to prevent the ends of their supporting pieces of wood from slipping on the cement floor, Mr. Clifford uttered an exclamation, then said:

"I have wrung my back badly. Help me to the tent. I must lie down."

Slowly and with great pain they staggered up the cave, Mr. Clifford leaning on Benita and a stick, till, reaching the tent at last, he almost fell on to the blankets and remained there practically crippled.

Now began Benita's terrible time, the worst of all her life. Every hour her father became more ill. Even before they took refuge in the cave he was completely broken down, and now after this accident he began to suffer very much. His rheumatism or sciatica, or whatever it was, seemed to settle upon the hurt muscles of his back, causing him so much pain that he could scarcely sleep for ten minutes at a stretch. Moreover, he would swallow but little of the rough food which was all Benita was able to prepare for him; nothing, indeed, except biscuit soaked in black coffee, which she boiled over a small fire made of wood that they had brought with them, and occasionally a little broth, tasteless stuff enough, for it was only the essence of biltong, or sun-dried flesh, flavoured with some salt.

Then there were two other terrors against she must fight, the darkness and the dread of Jacob Meyer. Perhaps the darkness was the worse of them. To live in that hideous gloom in which their single lamp, for she dared burn no more lest the oil should give out, seemed but as one star to the whole night, ah! who that had not endured it could know what it meant? There the sick man, yonder the grinning skeletons, around the blackness and the silence, and beyond these again a miserable death, or Jacob Meyer. But of him Benita saw nothing, though once or twice she thought that she heard his voice raving outside the wall which they had built. If so, either he did not try to pull it down, or he failed in the attempt, or perhaps he feared that should he succeed, he would be greeted by a bullet. So at last she gave up thinking about him. Should he force his way into the cave she must deal with the situation as best she could. Meanwhile, her father's strength was sinking fast.

Three awful days went by in this fashion, and the end drew near. Although she tried to force herself to it, Benita could not swallow enough food to keep up her strength. Now that the passage was closed the atmosphere of this old vault, for it was nothing more, thickened by the smoke of the fire which she was obliged to burn, grew poisonous and choked her. Want of sleep exhausted her, dread of what the morrow might bring forth crushed her strong spirit. She began to break down, knowing that the hour was near when she and her father must die together.

Once, as she slept awhile at his side, being wakened by his groaning, Benita looked at her watch. It was midnight. She rose, and going to the embers of the little fire, warmed up some of her biltong broth which she poured into a tin pannikin. With difficulty she forced him to swallow a few mouthfuls of it, then, feeling a sudden weakness, drank the rest herself. It gave her power to think, and her father dozed off into an uneasy sleep.

Alas! thinking was of no use, nothing could be done. There was no hope save in prayer. Restlessness seized Benita, and taking the lantern she wandered round the cave. The wall that they had built remained intact, and oh! to think that beyond it flowed the free air and shone the blessed stars! Back she came again, skirting the pits that Jacob Meyer had dug, and the grave of the old monk, till she reached the steps of the crucifix, and holding up her candle, looked at the thorn-crowned brow of the Christ above.

It was wonderfully carved; that dying face was full of pity. Would not He Whom it represented pity her? She knelt down on the topmost step, and clasping the pierced feet with her arms, began to pray earnestly, not for herself but that she might save her father. She prayed as she had never prayed before, and so praying, sank into a torpor or a swoon.

It seemed to Benita that this sleep of hers suddenly became alive; in it she saw many things. For instance, she saw herself seated in a state of trance upon that very step where now she knelt, while before her stood her father and Jacob Meyer. Moreover, something spoke in her; she could not hear a voice, but she seemed to see the words written in the air before her. These were the words:—

"*Clasp the feet of the Christ and draw them to the left. The passage beneath leads to the chamber where the gold is hid, and thence to the river bank. That is the secret which ere I depart, I the dead Benita, pass on to you, the living Benita, as I am commanded. In life and death peace be to your soul.*"

Thrice did this message appear to repeat itself in the consciousness of Benita. Then, suddenly as she had slept, she woke again with every letter of it imprinted on her mind. Doubtless it was a dream, nothing but a dream bred by the fact that her arms were clasping the feet of the crucifix. What did it say? "Draw them to the left."

She did so, but nothing stirred. Again she tried, and still nothing stirred. Of course it was a dream. Why had such been sent to mock her? In a kind of mad irritation she put out all her remaining strength and wrestled with those stony feet. *They moved a little*—then of a sudden, without any further effort on her part, swung round as high as the knees where drapery hung, concealing the join in them. Yes, they swung round, revealing the head of a stair, up which blew a cold wind that it was sweet to breathe.

Benita rose, gasping. Then she seized her lantern and ran to the little tent where her father lay.

XXII.
THE VOICE OF THE LIVING

Mr. Clifford was awake again now.

"Where have you been?" he asked querulously in a thin voice. "I wanted you." Then as the light from the candle shone upon it, he noted the change that had come over her pale face, and added: "What has happened? Is Meyer dead? Are we free?"

Benita shook her head. "He was alive a few hours ago, for I could hear him raving and shouting outside the wall we built. But, father, it has all come back to me; I believe that I have found it."

"What has come back? What have you found? Are you mad, too, like Jacob?"

"What something told me when I was in the trance which afterwards I forgot, but now remember. And I have found the passage which leads to where they hid the gold. It begins behind the crucifix, where no one ever thought of looking."

This matter of the gold did not seem to interest Mr. Clifford. In his state all the wealth beneath the soil of Africa would not have appealed to him. Moreover, he hated the name of that accursed treasure, which was bringing them to such a miserable end.

"Where does the passage run? Have you looked?" he asked.

"Not yet, but the voice in me said—I mean, I dreamed—that it goes down to the river-side. If you leant on me do you think that you could walk?"

"Not one inch," he answered. "Here where I am I shall die."

"No, no, don't talk like that. We may be saved now that I have found a way. Oh, if only you could—if only you could walk, or if I had the strength to carry you!" and she wrung her hands and began to weep, so weak was she.

Her father looked at her searchingly. Then he said:

"Well, love, I cannot, so there's an end. But you can, and you had better go."

"What! And leave you? Never."

"Yes, and leave me. Look, there is but a little oil left and only a few candles. The biscuits are done and neither of us can swallow that biltong any more. I suppose that I am dying, and your health and strength are failing you quickly in this darkness; if you stop here you must soon follow me. And what is the alternative? The madman outside—that is, if you could find strength to pull down the wall, which I doubt. You had best go, Benita."

But still she said she would not.

"Do you not see," he added, "that it is my only chance of life? If you go you may be able to bring me help before the end comes. Should there be a passage the probability is that, although they know nothing of it, it finishes somewhere by the wall of the first enclosure where the Makalanga are. If so, you may find the Molimo, or if he is dead, Tamas or one of the others, and they will help us. Go, Benita, go at once."

"I never thought of that," she answered in a changed voice. "Of course, it may be so, if the passage goes down at all. Well, at least I can look and come back to tell you."

Then Benita placed the remainder of the oil close by her father's side, so that he could refill the lamp, for the use of his hands still remained to him. Also, she set there such crumbs of biscuit as were left, some of the biltong, a flask of Hollands, and a pail of water. This done, she put on her long cloak, filled one of its pockets with biltong, and the other with matches and three of the four remaining candles. The fourth she insisted on leaving beside her father's bed. When everything was ready she knelt down at his side, kissed him, and from her heart put up a prayer that they might both live to meet again, although she knew well that this they could scarcely hope to do.

Had two people ever been in a more dreadful situation, she wondered, as she looked at her father lying there, whom she must leave to fight with Death alone in that awful place, while she went forth to meet him in the unknown bowels of the earth!

Mr. Clifford read her thoughts. "Yes," he said, "it is a strange parting and a wild errand. But who knows? It may please Providence to take you through, and if not—why, our troubles will soon be over."

Then once more they kissed, and not daring to try to speak, Benita tore herself away. Passing into the passage whereof the lower half of the crucifix formed the door, she paused for a moment to examine it and to place a fragment of rock in such fashion that it could not shut again behind her. Her idea was that it worked by aid of some spring, but now she saw that this was not so, as the whole mass hung upon three stone hinges beautifully concealed. The dust and corrosion of ages which had made this door so hard to open, by filling up the tiny spaces between it and its framework, had also rendered these cracks utterly imperceptible to the eye. So accurately was it fashioned, indeed, that no one who did not know its secret would have discovered it if they searched for months or years.

Though at the time Benita took little note of such details, the passage beyond and the stair descending from it showed the same perfect workmanship. Evidently this secret way dated not from the Portuguese period, but from that of the Phoenicians or other ancients, to whose treasure-chamber it was the approach, opening as it did from their holy of holies, to which none were admitted save the head priests. The passage, which was about seven feet high by four wide, had been hewn out of the live rock of the mountain, for thousands of little marks left by the workmen's chisels were still discernible upon its walls. So it was with the stair, that had been but little used, and remained fresh as the day when it was finished.

Down the steps, candle in hand, flitted Benita, counting them as she went. The thirtieth brought her to a landing. Here it was that she saw the first traces of that treasure which they had suffered so much to find. Something glittered at her feet. She picked it up. It was a little bar of gold weighing two or three ounces that doubtless had been dropped there. Throwing it down again she looked in front of her, and to her dismay saw a door of wood with iron bolts. But the bolts had never been shot, and when she pulled at it the door creaked upon its rusty hinges and opened. She was on the threshold of the treasure-chamber!

It was square and of the size of a small room, packed on either side almost to the low, vaulted roof with small bags of raw hide, carelessly arranged. Quite near to the door one of these bags had slipped down and burst open. It was filled with gold, some in ingots and some in raw nuggets, for there they lay in a shining, scattered heap. As she stooped to look it came into the mind of Benita that her father had said that in her trance she had told them that one of the bags of treasure was burst, and that the skin of which it had been made was black and red. Behold! before her lay the burst bag, and the colour of the hide was black and red.

She shivered. The thing was uncanny, terrible. Uncanny was it also to see in the thick dust, which in the course of twenty or more of centuries had gathered on the floor, the mark of footprints, those of the last persons who had visited this place. There had been two of them, a man and a woman, and they were no savages, for they wore shoes. Benita placed her foot in the print left by that dead woman. It filled it exactly, it might have been her own. Perhaps, she thought to herself, that other Benita had descended here with her father, after the Portuguese had hidden away their wealth, that she might be shown where it was, and of what it consisted.

One more glance at all this priceless, misery-working gold, and on she went, she who was seeking the gold of life and liberty for herself and him who lay above. Supposing that the stairway ended there? She stopped, she looked round, but could see no other door. To see the better she halted and opened the glass of her lantern. Still she could perceive nothing, and her heart sank. Yet why did the candle flicker so fiercely? And why was the air in this deep place so fresh? She walked forward a pace or two, then noticed suddenly that those footprints of the dead that she was following disappeared immediately in front of her, and she stopped.

It was but just in time. One step more and she would have fallen down the mouth of a deep pit. Once it had been covered with a stone, but this stone was removed, and had never been replaced. Look! there it stood against the wall of the chamber. Well was this for Benita, since her frail strength would not have sufficed to stir that massive block, even if she had discovered its existence beneath the dust.

Now she saw that down the pit ran another ladderlike stair of stone, very narrow and precipitous. Without hesitation she began its descent. Down she went and down—one hundred steps, two hundred steps, two hundred and seventy-five steps, and all the way wherever the dust had gathered the man's and the woman's footprints ran before her. There was a double line of them, one line going down and the other line returning. Those that returned were the last, for often they appeared over those that descended. Why had these dead people returned, Benita wondered.

The stair had ended; now she was in a kind of natural cave, for its sides and roof were rugged; moreover, water trickled and dripped from them. It was not very large, and it smelt horribly of mud and other things. Again she searched by the feeble light of her candle, but could see no exit. Suddenly she saw something else, however, for stepping on what she took to be a rock, to her horror it moved beneath her. She heard a snap as of jaws, a violent blow upon the leg nearly knocked her off her feet, and as she staggered backwards she saw a huge and loathsome shape rushing away into the darkness. The rock that she had trodden on was a crocodile which had its den here! With a little scream she retreated to her stair. Death she had expected—but to be eaten by crocodiles!

Yet as Benita stood there panting a blessed hope rose in her breast. If a crocodile came in there it must also get out, and where such a great creature could go, a woman would be able to follow. Also, she must be near the water, since otherwise it could never have chosen this hole for its habitation. She collected her courage, and having clapped her hands and waved the lantern about to scare any alligators that might still be lurking there, hearing and seeing nothing more, she descended to where she had trodden upon the reptile. Evidently this was its bed, for its long body had left an impress upon the mud, and all about lay the remains of creatures that it had brought in for food. Moreover, a path ran outwards, its well-worn trail distinct even in that light.

She followed this path, which ended apparently in a blank wall. Then it was that Benita guessed why those dead folks' footprints had returned, for here had been a doorway which in some past age those who used it built up with blocks of stone and cement. How, then, did the crocodile get out? Stooping down she searched, and perceived, a few yards to the right of the door, a hole that looked as though it were water-worn. Now Benita thought that she understood. The rock was softer here, and centuries of flood had eaten it away, leaving a crack in the stratum which the crocodiles had found out and enlarged. Down she went on her hands and knees, and thrusting the lantern in front of her, crept along that noisome drain, for this was what it resembled. And now—oh! now she felt air blowing in her face, and heard the sound of reeds whispering, and water running, and saw hanging like a lamp in the blue sky, a star—the morning star! Benita could have wept, she could have worshipped it, yet she pushed on between rocks till she found herself among tall reeds, and standing in water. She had gained the banks of the Zambesi.

Instantly, by instinct as it were, Benita extinguished her candle, fearing lest it should betray her, for constant danger had made her very cunning. The dawn had not yet broken, but the waning moon and the stars gave a good light. She paused to look. There above her towered the outermost wall of Bambatse, against which the river washed, except at such times as the present, when it was very low.

So she was not in the fortress as she had hoped, but without it, and oh! what should she do? Go back again? How would that serve her father or herself? Go on? Then she might fall into the hands of the Matabele whose camp was a little lower down, as from her perch upon the top of the cone she had seen that poor white man do. Ah! the white man! If only he lived and she could reach him! Perhaps they had not killed him after all. It was madness, yet she would try to discover; something impelled her to take the risk. If she failed and escaped, perhaps then she might call to the Makalanga, and they would let down a rope and draw her up the wall before the Matabele caught her. She would not go back empty-handed, to die in that dreadful place with her poor father. Better perish here in the sweet air and beneath the stars, even if it were upon a Matabele spear, or by a bullet from her own pistol.

She looked about her to take her bearings in case it should ever be necessary for her to return to the entrance of the cave. This proved easy, for a hundred or so feet above her—where the sheer face of the cliff jutted out a little, at that very spot indeed on which tradition said that the body of the Señora da Ferreira had struck in its fall, and the necklace Benita wore to-day was torn from her—a stunted mimosa grew in some cleft of the rock. To mark the crocodile run itself she bent down a bunch of reeds, and having first lit a few Tandstickor brimstone matches and thrown them about inside of it, that the smell of them might scare the beast should it wish to return, she set her lantern behind a stone near to the mouth of the hole.

Then Benita began her journey which, when the river was high, it would not have been possible for her to make except by swimming. As it was, a margin of marsh was left between her and the steep, rocky side of the mount from which the great wall rose, and through this she made her way. Never was she likely to forget that walk. The tall reeds dripped their dew upon her until she was soaked; long, black-tailed finches—saccaboolas the natives call them—flew up undisturbed, and lobbed away across the river; owls flitted past and bitterns boomed at the coming of the dawn. Great fish splashed also in the shallows, or were they crocodiles? Benita hoped not—for one day she had seen enough of crocodiles.

It was all very strange. Could she be the same woman, she wondered, who not a year before had been walking with her cousins down Westbourne Grove, and studying Whiteley's windows? What would these cousins say now if they could see her, white-faced, large-eyed, desperate, splashing through the mud upon the unknown banks of the Zambesi, flying from death to death!

On she struggled, above her the pearly sky in which the stars were fading, around her the wet reeds, and pervading all the heavy low-lying mists of dawn. She was past the round of the walls, and at length stood upon dry ground where the Matabele had made their camp. But in that fog she saw no Matabele; probably their fires were out, and she chanced to pass between the sentries. Instinctively, more than by reason, she headed for that hillock upon which she had seen the white man's waggon, in the vague hope that it might still be there. On she struggled, still on, till at length she blundered against something soft and warm, and perceived that it was an ox tied to a trek-tow, beyond which were other oxen and a white waggon-cap.

So it *was* still there! But the white man, where was he? Through the dense mist Benita crept to the disselboom. Then, seeing and hearing nothing, she climbed to the voorkissie and kneeling on it, separated the tent flaps and peered into the waggon. Still she could see nothing because of the mist, yet she heard something, a man breathing in his sleep. Somehow she thought that it was a white man; a Kaffir did not breathe like that. She did not know what to do, so remained kneeling there. It seemed as though the man who was asleep began to feel her presence, for he muttered to himself—surely the words were English! Then quite suddenly he struck a match and lit a candle which stood in a beer bottle by his side. She could not see his face while he lit the match, for his arm hid it, and the candle burned up slowly. Then the first thing she saw was the barrel of a revolver pointing straight at her.

"Now, my black friend," said a pleasant voice, "down you go or I shoot. One, two! Oh, my God!"

The candle burned up, its light fell upon the white, elfish face of Benita, whose long dark hair streamed about her; it shone in her great eyes. Still she could see nothing, for it dazzled her.

"Oh, my God!" said the voice again. "Benita! Benita! Have you come to tell me that I must join you? Well, I am ready, my sweet, my sweet! Now I shall hear your answer."

"Yes," she whispered, and crawling forward down the cartel Benita fell upon his breast.

For she knew him at last—dead or living she cared not—she knew him, and out of hell crept to him, her heaven and her home!

XXIII.
BENITA GIVES HER ANSWER

"Your answer, Benita," Robert said dreamily, for to him this thing seemed a dream.

"Have I not given it, months ago? Oh, I remember, it was only in my heart, not on my lips, when that blow fell on me! Then afterwards I heard what you had done and I nearly died. I wished that I might die to be with you, but I could not. I was too strong; now I understand the reason. Well, it seems that we are both living, and whatever happens, here is my answer, if it is worth anything to you. Once and for all, I love you. I am not ashamed to say it, because very soon we may be separated for the last time. But I cannot talk now, I have come here to save my father."

"Where is he, Benita?"

"Dying in a cave up at the top of that fortress. I got down by a secret way. Are the Matabele still here?"

"Very much so," he answered. "But something has happened. My guard woke me an hour ago to say that a messenger had arrived from their king, Lobengula, and now they are talking over the message. That is how you came to get through, otherwise the sentries would have assegaied you, the brutes," and he drew her to him and kissed her passionately for the first time; then, as though ashamed of himself, let her go.

"Have you anything to eat?" she asked. "I—I—am starving. I didn't feel it before, but now — —"

"Starving, you starving, while I—look, here is some cold meat which I could not get down last night, and put by for the Kaffirs. Great Heavens! that I should feed you with Kaffirs' leavings! But it is good—eat it."

Benita took the stuff in her fingers and swallowed it greedily; she who for days had lived on nothing but a little biscuit and biltong. It tasted delicious to her—never had she eaten anything so good. And all the while he watched her with glowing eyes.

"How can you look at me?" she said at length. "I must be horrible; I have been living in the dark and crawling through mud. I trod upon a crocodile!" and she shuddered.

"Whatever you are I never want to see you different," he answered slowly. "To me you are most beautiful."

Even then, wreck as she was, the poor girl flushed, and there was a mist in her eyes as she looked up and said:

"Thank you. I don't care now what happens to me, and what has happened doesn't matter at all. But can we get away?"

"I don't know," he answered; "but I doubt it. Go and sit on the waggon-box for a few minutes while I dress, and we will see."

Benita went. The mist was thinning now, and through it she saw a sight at which her heart sank, for between her and the mount Bambatse Matabele were pouring towards their camp on the river's edge. They were cut off. A couple of minutes later Robert joined her, and as he came she looked at him anxiously in the growing light. He seemed older than when they had parted on the *Zanzibar*; changed, too, for now his face was serious, and he had grown a beard; also, he appeared to limp.

"I am afraid there is an end," she said, pointing to the Matabele below.

"Yes, it looks like it. But like you, I say, what does it matter now?" and he took her hand in his, adding: "let us be happy while we can if only for a few minutes. They will be here presently."

"What are you?" she asked. "A prisoner?"

"That's it. I was following you when they captured me; for I have been here before and knew the way. They were going to kill me on general principles, only it occurred to one of them who was more intelligent than the rest that I, being a white man, might be able to show them how to storm the place. Now I was sure that you were there, for I saw you standing on that point, though they thought you were the Spirit of Bambatse. So I wasn't anxious to help them, for then—you know what happens when the Matabele are the stormers! But—as you still lived—I wasn't anxious to die either. So I set them to work to dig a hole with their assegais and sharp axes, through granite. They have completed exactly twenty feet of it, and I reckon that there are one hundred and forty to go. Last night they got tired of that tunnel and talked of killing me again, unless I could show them a better plan. Now all the fat is in the fire, and I don't know what is to happen. Hullo! here they come. Hide in the waggon, quick!"

Benita obeyed, and from under cover of the tent where the Matabele could not see her, watched and listened. The party that approached consisted of a chief and about twenty men, who marched behind him as a guard. Benita knew that chief. He was the captain Maduna, he of the royal blood whose life she had saved. By his side was a Natal Zulu, Robert Seymour's driver, who could speak English and acted as interpreter.

"White man," said Maduna, "a message has reached us from our king. Lobengula makes a great war and has need of us. He summons us back from this petty fray, this fight against cowards who hide behind walls, whom otherwise we would have killed, everyone, yes, if we sat here till we grew old. So for this time we leave them alone."

Robert answered politely that he was glad to hear it, and wished them a good journey.

"Wish yourself a good journey, white man," was the stern reply.

"Why? Do you desire that I should accompany you to Lobengula?"

"No, you go before us to the kraal of the Black One who is even greater than the child of Moselikatse, to that king who is called Death."

Robert crossed his arms and said: "Say on."

"White man, I promised you life if you would show us how to pierce or climb those walls. But you have made fools of us—you have set us to cut through rock with spears and axes. Yes, to hoe at rock as though it were soil—you who with the wisdom of your people could have taught us some better way. Therefore we must go back to our king disgraced, having failed in his service, and therefore you who have mocked us shall die. Come down now, that we may kill you quietly, and learn whether or no you are a brave man."

Then it was, while her lover's hand was moving towards the pistol hidden beneath his coat, that Benita, with a quick movement, emerged from the waggon in which she crouched, and stood up at his side upon the driving box.

"*Ow!*" said the Captain. "It is the White Maiden. Now how came she here? Surely this is great magic. Can a woman fly like a bird?" and they stared at her amazed.

"What does it matter how I came, chief Maduna?" she answered in Zulu. "Yet I will tell you why I came. It was to save you from dipping your spear in the innocent blood, and bringing on your head the curse of the innocent blood. Answer me now. Who gave you and your brother yonder your lives within that wall when the Makalanga would have torn you limb from limb, as hyenas tear a buck? Was it I or another?"

"Inkosi-kaas—Chieftainess," replied the great Captain, raising his broad spear in salute. "It was you and no other."

"And what did you promise me then, Prince Maduna?"

"Maiden of high birth, I promised you your life and your goods, should you ever fall into my power."

"Does a leader of the Amandabele, one of the royal blood, lie like a Mashona or a Makalanga slave? Does he do worse—tell half the truth only, like a cheat who buys and keeps back half the price?" she asked contemptuously. "Maduna, you promised me not one life, but two, two lives and the goods that belong to both. Ask of your brother there, who was witness of the words."

"Great Heavens!" muttered Robert Seymour to himself, as he looked at Benita standing with outstretched hand and flashing eyes. "Who would have thought that a starved woman could play such a part with death on the hazard?"

"It is as this daughter of white chiefs says," answered the man to whom she had appealed. "When she freed us from the fangs of those dogs, you promised her two lives, my brother, one for yours and one for mine."

"Hear him," went on Benita. "He promised me two lives, and how did this prince of the royal blood keep his promise? When I and the old man, my father, rode hence in peace, he loosed his spears upon us; he hunted us. Yet it was the hunters who fell into the trap, not the hunted."

"Maiden," replied Maduna, in a shamed voice, "that was your fault, not mine. If you had appealed to me I would have let you go. But you killed my sentry, and then the chase began, and ere I knew who you were my runners were out of call."

"Little time had I to ask your mercy; but so be it," said Benita. "I accept your word, and I forgive you that offence. Now fulfil your oath. Begone and leave us in peace."

Still Maduna hesitated.

"I must make report to the king," he said. "What is this white man to you that I should spare him? I give you your life and your father's life, not that of this white man who has tricked us. If he were your father, or your brother, it would be otherwise. But he is a stranger, and belongs to me, not to you."

"Maduna," she asked, "do women such as I am share the waggon of a stranger? This man is more to me than father or brother. He is my husband, and I claim his life."

"*Ow!*" said the spokesman of the audience, "we understand now. She is his wife, and has a right to him. If she were not his wife she would not be in his waggon. It is plain that she speaks the truth, though how she came here we do not know, unless, as we think, she is a witch," and he smiled at his own cleverness.

"Inkosi-kaas," said Maduna, "you have persuaded me. I give you the life of that white fox, your husband, and I hope that he will not trick you as he has tricked us, and set you to hoe rock instead of soil," and he looked at Robert wrathfully. "I give him to you and all his belongings. Now, is there anything else that you would ask?"

"Yes," replied Benita coolly, "you have many oxen there which you took from the other Makalanga. Mine are eaten and I need cattle to draw my waggon. I ask a present of twenty of them, and," she added by an afterthought, "two cows with young calves, for my father is sick yonder, and must have milk."

"Oh! give them to her. Give them to her," said Maduna, with a tragic gesture that in any other circumstances would have made Benita laugh. "Give them to her and see that they are good ones, before she asks our shields and spears also—for after all she saved my life."

So men departed to fetch those cows and oxen, which presently were driven in.

While this talk was in progress the great impi of the Matabele was massing for the march, on the flat ground a little to the right of them. Now they began to come past in companies, preceded by the lads who carried the mats and cooking-pots and drove the captured sheep and cattle. By this time the story of Benita, the witch-woman whom they could not kill, and who had mysteriously flown from the top of the peak into their prisoner's waggon, had spread among them. They knew also that it was she who had saved their general from the Makalanga, and those who had heard her admired the wit and courage with which she had pleaded and won her cause. Therefore, as they marched past in their companies, singing a song of abuse and defiance of the Makalanga who peered at them from the top of the wall, they lifted their great spears in salutation to Benita standing upon the waggon-box.

Indeed, they were a wondrous and imposing spectacle, such a one as few white women have ever seen.

At length all were gone except Maduna and a body-guard of two hundred men. He walked to the front of the waggon and addressed Robert Seymour.

"Listen, you fox who set us to hoe granite," he said indignantly. "You have outwitted us this time, but if ever I meet you again, then you die. Now I have given you your life, but," he added, almost pleadingly, "if you are really brave as white men are said to be, will you not come down and fight me man to man for honour's sake?"

"I think not," answered Robert, when he understood this challenge, "for what chance should I have against so brave a warrior? Also this lady—my wife—needs my help on her journey home."

Maduna turned from him contemptuously to Benita.

"I go," he said, "and fear not; you will meet no Matabele on that journey. Have you more words for me, O Beautiful One, with a tongue of oil and a wit that cuts like steel?"

"Yes," answered Benita. "You have dealt well with me, and in reward I give you of my good luck. Bear this message to your king from the White Witch of Bambatse, for I am she and no other. That he leave these Makalanga, my servants, to dwell unharmed in their ancient home, and that he lift no spear against the White Men, lest that evil which the Molimo foretold to you, should fall upon him."

"Ah!" said Maduna, "now I understand how you flew from the mountain top into this man's waggon. You are not a white woman, you are the ancient Witch of Bambatse herself. You have said it, and with such it is not well to war. Great lady of Magic, Spirit from of old, I salute you, and I thank you for your gifts of life and fortune. Farewell."

Then he, too, stalked away at the head of his guard, so that presently, save for the three Zulu servants and the herd of cattle, Robert and Benita were left utterly alone.

Now, her part played and the victory won, Benita burst into tears and fell upon her lover's breast.

Presently she remembered, and freed herself from his arms.

"I am a selfish wretch," she said. "How dare I be so happy when my father is dead or dying? We must go at once."

"Go where?" asked the bewildered Robert.

"To the top of the mountain, of course, whence I came. Oh! please don't stop to question me, I'll tell you as we walk. Stay," and she called to the Zulu driver, who with an air of utter amazement was engaged in milking one of the gift cows, to fill two bottles with the milk.

"Had we not better shout to the Makalanga to let us in?" suggested Robert, while this was being done, and Benita wrapped some cooked meat in a cloth.

"No, no. They will think I am what I said I was—the Witch of Bambatse, whose appearance heralds misfortune, and fear a trap. Besides, we could not climb the top wall. You must follow my road, and if you can trust them, bring two of those men with you with lanterns. The lad can stop to herd the cattle."

Three minutes later, followed by the two Zulus, they were walking—or rather, running—along the banks of the Zambesi.

"Why do you not come quicker?" she asked impatiently. "Oh, I beg your pardon, you are lame. Robert, what made you lame, and oh! why are you not dead, as they all swore you were, you, you—hero, for I know that part of the story?"

"For a very simple reason, Benita: because I didn't die. When that Kaffir took the watch from me I was insensible, that's all. The sun brought me to life afterwards. Then some natives turned up, good people in their way, although I could not understand a word they said. They made a stretcher of boughs and carried me for some miles to their kraal inland. It hurt awfully, for my thigh was broken, but I arrived at last. There a Kaffir doctor set my leg in his own fashion; it has left it an inch shorter than the other, but that's better than nothing.

"In that place I lay for two solid months, for there was no white man within a hundred miles, and if there had been I could not have communicated with him. Afterwards I spent another month limping up towards Natal, until I could buy a horse. The rest is very short. Hearing of my reported death, I came as fast as I could to your father's farm, Rooi Krantz, where I learned from the old vrouw Sally that you had taken to treasure-hunting, the same treasure that I told you of on the *Zanzibar*.

"So I followed your spoor, met the servants whom you had sent back, who told me all about you, and in due course, after many adventures, as they say in a book, walked into the camp of our friends, the Matabele.

"They were going to kill me at once, when suddenly you appeared upon that point of rock, glittering like—like the angel of the dawn. I knew that it must be you, for I had found out about your attempted escape, and how you were hunted back to this place. But the Matabele all thought that it was the Spirit of Bambatse, who has a great reputation in these parts. Well, that took off their attention, and afterwards, as I told you, it occurred to them that I might be an engineer. You know the rest, don't you?"

"Yes," answered Benita softly. "I know the rest."

Then they plunged into the reeds and were obliged to stop talking, since they must walk in single file. Presently Benita looked up and saw that she was under the thorn which grew in the cleft of the rock. Also, with some trouble she found the bunch of reeds that she had bent down, to mark the inconspicuous hole through which she had crept, and by it her lantern. It seemed weeks since she had left it there.

"Now," she said, "light your candles, and if you see a crocodile, please shoot."

XXIV.
THE TRUE GOLD

"Let me go first," said Robert.

"No," answered Benita. "I know the way; but please do watch for that horrible crocodile."

Then she knelt down and crept into the hole, while after her came Robert, and after him the two Zulus, who protested that they were not ant-bears to burrow under ground. Lifting the lantern she searched the cave, and as she could see no signs of the crocodile, walked on boldly to where the stair began.

"Be quick," she whispered to Robert, for in that place it seemed natural to speak low. "My father is above and near his death. I am dreadfully afraid lest we should be too late."

So they toiled up the endless steps, a very strange procession, for the two Zulus, bold men enough outside, were shaking with fright, till at length Benita clambered out of the trap door on to the floor of the treasure chamber, and turned to help Robert, whose lameness made him somewhat slow and awkward.

"What's all that?" he asked, pointing to the hide sacks, while they waited for the two scared Kaffirs to join them.

"Oh!" she answered indifferently, "gold, I believe. Look, there is some of it on the floor, over Benita da Ferreira's footsteps."

"Gold! Why, it must be worth——! And who on earth is Benita da Ferreira?"

"I will tell you afterwards. She has been dead two or three hundred years; it was her gold, or her people's, and those are her footprints in the dust. How stupid you are not to understand! Never mind the hateful stuff; come on quickly."

So they passed the door which she had opened that morning, and clambered up the remaining stairway. So full was Benita of terrors that she could never remember how she climbed them. Suppose that the foot of the crucifix had swung to; suppose that her father were dead; suppose that Jacob Meyer had broken into the cave? Well for herself she was no longer afraid of Jacob Meyer. Oh, they were there! The heavy door *had* begun to close, but mercifully her bit of rock kept it ajar.

"Father! Father!" she cried, running towards the tent.

No answer came. She threw aside the flap, held down the lantern and looked. There he lay, white and still. She was too late!

"He is dead, he is dead!" she wailed. Robert knelt down at her side, and examined the old man, while she waited in an agony.

"He ought to be," he said slowly; "but, Benita, I don't think he is. I can feel his heart stir. No, don't stop to talk. Pour out some of that squareface, and here, mix it with this milk."

She obeyed, and while he held up her father's head, with a trembling hand emptied a little of the drink into his mouth. At first it ran out again, then almost automatically he swallowed some, and they knew that he was alive, and thanked Heaven. Ten minutes later Mr. Clifford was sitting up staring at them with dull and wondering eyes, while outside the two Zulus, whose nerves had now utterly broken down, were contemplating the pile of skeletons in the corner and the white towering crucifix, and loudly lamenting that they should have been brought to perish in this place of bones and ghosts.

"Is it Jacob Meyer who makes that noise?" asked Mr. Clifford faintly. "And, Benita, where have you been so long, and—who is this gentleman with you? I seem to remember his face."

"He is the white man who was in the waggon, father, an old friend come to life again. Robert, can't you stop the howling of those Kaffirs? Though I am sure I don't wonder that they howl; I should have liked to do so for days. Oh! father, father, don't you understand me? We are saved, yes, snatched out of hell and the jaws of death."

"Is Jacob Meyer dead, then?" he asked.

"I don't know where he is or what has happened to him, and I don't care, but perhaps we had better find out. Robert, there is a madman outside. Make the Kaffirs pull down that wall, would you? and catch him."

"What wall? What madman?" he asked, staring at her.

"Oh, of course you don't know that, either. You know nothing. I'll show you, and you must be prepared, for probably he will shoot at us."

"It all sounds a little risky, doesn't it?" asked Robert doubtfully.

"Yes, but we must take the risk. We cannot carry my father down that place, and unless we can get him into light and air soon, he will certainly die. The man outside is Jacob Meyer, his partner—you remember him. All these weeks of hardship and treasure-hunting have sent him off his head, and he wanted to mesmerize me and——"

"And what? Make love to you?"

She nodded, then went on:

"So when he could not get his way about the mesmerism and so forth, he threatened to murder my father, and that is why we had to hide in this cave and build ourselves up, till at last I found the way out."

"Amiable gentleman, Mr. Jacob Meyer, now as always," said Robert flushing. "To think that you should have been in the power of a scoundrel like that! Well, I hope to come square with him."

"Don't hurt him, dear, unless you are obliged. Remember he is not responsible. He thought he saw a ghost here the other day."

"Unless he behaves himself he is likely to see a good many soon," muttered Robert.

Then they went down the cave, and as silently as possible began to work at the wall, destroying in a few minutes what had been built up with so much labour. When it was nearly down the Zulus were told that there was an enemy outside, and that they must help to catch him if necessary, but were not to harm him. They assented gladly enough; indeed, to get out of that cave they would have faced half a dozen enemies.

Now there was a hole right through the wall, and Robert bade Benita stand to one side. Then as soon as his eyes became accustomed to the little light that penetrated there, he drew his revolver and beckoned the Kaffirs to follow. Down the passage they crept, slowly, lest they should be blinded when they came to the glare of the sunshine, while Benita waited with a beating heart.

A little time went by, she never knew how long, till suddenly a rifle shot rang through the stillness. Benita was able to bear no more. She rushed down the winding passage, and presently, just beyond its mouth, in a blurred and indistinct fashion saw that the two white men were rolling together on the ground, while the Kaffirs sprang round watching for an opportunity to seize one of them. At that moment they succeeded, and Robert rose, dusting his hands and knees.

"Amiable gentleman, Mr. Jacob Meyer," he repeated. "I could have killed him as his back was towards me, but didn't because you asked me not. Then I stumbled with my lame leg, and he whipped round and let drive with his rifle. Look," and he showed her where the bullet had cut his ear. "Luckily I got hold of him before he could loose off another."

Benita could find no words, her heart was too full of thankfulness. Only she seized Robert's hand and kissed it. Then she looked at Jacob.

He was lying upon the broad of his back, the two big Zulus holding his arms and legs; his lips were cracked, blue and swollen; his face was almost black, but his eyes still shone bright with insanity and hate.

"I know you," he screamed hoarsely to Robert. "You are another ghost, the ghost of that man who was drowned. Otherwise my bullet would have killed you."

"Yes, Mr. Meyer," Seymour answered, "I am a ghost. Now, you boys, here's a bit of rope. Tie his hands behind his back and search him. There is a pistol in that pocket."

They obeyed, and presently Meyer was disarmed and bound fast to a tree.

"Water," he moaned. "For days I have had nothing but the dew I could lick off the leaves."

Pitying his plight, Benita ran into the cave and returned presently with a tin of water. One of the Kaffirs held it to his lips, and he drank greedily. Then, leaving one Zulu to watch him, Robert, Benita, and the other Zulu went back, and as gently as they could carried out Mr. Clifford on his mattress, placing him in the shade of a rock, where he lay blessing them feebly, because they had brought him into the light again. At the sight of the old man Meyer's rage blazed up afresh.

"Ah," he screamed, "if only I had killed you long ago, she would be mine now, not that fellow's. It was you who stood between us."

"Look here, my friend," broke in Robert. "I forgive you everything else, but, mad or sane, be good enough to keep Miss Clifford's name off your lips, or I will hand you over to those Kaffirs to be dealt with as you deserve."

Then Jacob understood, and was silent. They gave him more water and food to eat, some of the meat that they had brought with them, which he devoured ravenously.

"Are you sensible now?" asked Robert when he had done. "Then listen to me; I have some good news for you. That treasure you have been hunting for has been found. We are going to give you half of it, one of the waggons and some oxen, and clear you out of this place. Then if I set eyes on you again before we get to a civilized country, I shoot you like a dog."

"You lie!" said Meyer sullenly. "You want to turn me out into the wilderness to be murdered by the Makalanga or the Matabele."

"Very well," said Robert. "Untie him, boys, and bring him along. I will show him whether I lie."

"Where are they taking me to?" asked Meyer. "Not into the cave? I won't go into the cave; it is haunted. If it hadn't been for the ghost there I would have broken down their wall long ago, and killed that old snake before her eyes. Whenever I went near that wall I saw it watching me."

"First time I ever heard of a ghost being useful," remarked Robert. "Bring him along. No, Benita, he shall see whether I am a liar."

So the lights were lit, and the two stalwart Zulus hauled Jacob forward, Robert and Benita following. At first he struggled violently, then, on finding that he could not escape, went on, his teeth chattering with fear.

"It is cruel," remonstrated Benita.

"A little cruelty will not do him any harm," Robert answered. "He has plenty to spare for other people. Besides, he is going to get what he has been looking for so long."

They led Jacob to the foot of the crucifix, where a paroxysm seemed to seize him, then pushed him through the swinging doorway beneath, and down the steep stairs, till once more they all stood in the treasure-chamber.

"Look," said Robert, and, drawing his hunting-knife, he slashed one of the hide bags, whereon instantly there flowed out a stream of beads and nuggets. "Now, my friend, am I a liar?" he asked.

At this wondrous sight Jacob's terror seemed to depart from him, and he grew cunning.

"Beautiful, beautiful!" he said, "more than I thought—sacks and sacks of gold. I shall be a king indeed. No, no, it is all a dream—like the rest. I don't believe it's there. Loose my arms and let me feel it."

"Untie him," said Robert, at the same time drawing his pistol and covering the man; "he can't do us any hurt."

The Kaffirs obeyed, and Jacob, springing at the slashed bag, plunged his thin hands into it.

"No lie," he screamed, "no lie," as he dragged the stuff out and smelt at it. "Gold, gold, gold! Hundreds of thousands of pounds' worth of gold! Let's make a bargain, Englishman, and I won't kill you as I meant to do. You take the girl and give me all the gold," and in his ecstasy he began to pour the glittering ingots over his head and body.

"A new version of the tale of Danaë," began Robert in a sarcastic voice, then suddenly paused, for a change had come over Jacob's face, a terrible change.

It turned ashen beneath the tan, his eyes grew large and round, he put up his hands as though to thrust something from him, his whole frame shivered, and his hair seemed to erect itself. Slowly he retreated backwards, and would have fallen down the unclosed trap-hole had not one of the Kaffirs pushed him away. Back he went, still back, till he struck the further wall and stood there, perhaps for half a minute. He lifted his hand and pointed first to those ancient footprints, some of which still remained in the dust of the floor, and next, as they thought, at Benita. His lips moved fast, he seemed to be pleading, remonstrating, yet—and this was the ghastliest part of it—from them there came no sound. Lastly, his eyes rolled up until only the whites of them were visible, his face became wet as though water had been poured over it, and, still without a sound, he fell forward and moved no more.

So terrible was the scene that with a howl of fear the two Kaffirs turned and fled up the stairway. Robert sprang to the Jew, dragged him over on to his back, put his hand upon his breast and lifted his eyelids.

"Dead," he said. "Stone dead. Privation, brain excitement, heart failure—that's the story."

"Perhaps," answered Benita faintly; "but really I think that I begin to believe in ghosts also. Look, I never noticed them before, and I didn't walk there, but those footsteps seem to lead right up to him." Then she turned too and fled.

Another week had gone by. The waggons were laden with a burden more precious perhaps than waggons have often borne before. In one of them, on a veritable bed of gold, slept Mr. Clifford, still very weak and ill, but somewhat better than he had been, and with a good prospect of recovery, at any rate for a while. They were to trek a little after dawn, and already Robert and Benita were up and waiting. She touched his arm and said to him:

"Come with me. I have a fancy to see that place once more, for the last time."

So they climbed the hill and the steep steps in the topmost wall that Meyer had blocked—re-opened now—and reaching the mouth of the cave, lit the lamps which they had brought with them, and entered. There were the fragments of the barricade that Benita had built with desperate hands, there was the altar of sacrifice standing cold and grey as it had stood for perhaps three thousand years. There was the tomb of the old monk who had a companion now, for in it Jacob Meyer lay with him, his bones covered by the *débris* that he himself had dug out in his mad search for wealth; and there the white Christ hung awful on His cross. Only the skeletons of the Portuguese were gone, for with the help of his Kaffirs Robert had moved them every one into the empty treasure-chamber, closing the trap beneath, and building up the door above, so that there they might lie in peace at last.

In this melancholy place they tarried but a little while, then, turning their backs upon it for ever, went out and climbed the granite cone to watch the sun rise over the broad Zambesi. Up it came in glory, that same sun which had shone upon the despairing Benita da

Ferreira, and upon the English Benita when she had stood there in utter hopelessness, and seen the white man captured by the Matabele.

Now, different was their state indeed, and there in that high place, whence perhaps many a wretched creature had been cast to death, whence certainly the Portuguese maiden had sought her death, these two happy beings were not ashamed to give thanks to Heaven for the joy which it had vouchsafed to them, and for their hopes of life full and long to be travelled hand in hand. Behind them was the terror of the cave, beneath them were the mists of the valley, but above them the light shone and rolled and sparkled, and above them stretched the eternal sky!

They descended the pillar, and near the foot of it saw an old man sitting. It was Mambo, the Molimo of the Makalanga: even when they were still far away from him they knew his snow-white head and thin, ascetic face. As they drew near Benita perceived that his eyes were closed, and whispered to Robert that he was asleep. Yet he had heard them coming, and even guessed her thought.

"Maiden," he said in his gentle voice, "maiden who soon shall be a wife, I do not sleep, although I dream of you as I have dreamt before. What did I say to you that day when first we met? That for you I had good tidings; that though death was all about you, you need not fear; that in this place you who had known great sorrow should find happiness and rest. Yet, maiden, you would not believe the words of the Munwali, spoken by his prophet's lips, as he at your side, who shall be your husband, would not believe me in years past when I told him that we should meet again."

"Father," she answered, "I thought your rest was that which we find only in the grave."

"You would not believe," he went on without heeding her, "and therefore you tried to fly, and therefore your heart was torn with terror and with agony, when it should have waited for the end in confidence and peace."

"Father, my trial was very sore."

"Maiden, I know it, and because it was so sore that patient Spirit of Bambatse bore with you, and through it all guided your feet aright. Yes, with you has that Spirit gone, by day, by night, in the morning and in the evening. Who was it that smote the man who lies dead yonder with horror and with madness when he would have bent your will to his and made you a wife to him? Who was it that told you the secret of the treasure-pit, and what footsteps went before you down its stair? Who was it that led you past the sentries of the Amandabele and gave you wit and power to snatch your lord's life from Maduna's bloody hand? Yes, with you it has gone and with you it will go. No more shall the White Witch stand upon the pillar point at the rising of the sun, or in the shining of the moon."

"Father, I have never understood you, and I do not understand you now," said Benita. "What has this spirit to do with me?"

He smiled a little, then answered slowly:

"That I may not tell you; that you shall learn one day, but never here. When you also have entered into silence, then you shall learn. But I say to you that this shall not be till your hair is as white as mine, and your years are as many. Ah! you thought that I had deserted you, when fearing for your father's life you wept and prayed in the darkness of the cave. Yet it was not so, for I did but suffer the doom which I had read to fulfil itself as it must do."

He rose to his feet and, resting on his staff, laid one withered hand upon the head of Benita.

"Maiden," he said, "we meet no more beneath the sun. Yet because you have brought deliverance to my people, because you are sweet and pure and true, take with you the blessing of Munwali, spoken by the mouth of his servant Mambo, the old Molimo of Bambatse. Though from time to time you must know tears and walk in the shade of sorrows, long and happy shall be your days with him whom you have chosen. Children shall spring up about you, and children's children, and with them also shall the blessing go. The gold you white folk love is yours, and it shall multiply and give food to the hungry and raiment to those that are a-cold. Yet in your own heart lies a richer store that cannot melt away, the countless treasure of mercy and of love. When you sleep and when you wake Love shall take you by the hand, till at length he leads you through life's dark cave to that eternal house of purest gold which soon or late those that seek it shall inherit," and with his staff he pointed to the glowing morning sky wherein one by one little rosy clouds floated upwards and were lost.

To Robert and to Benita's misty eyes they looked like bright-winged angels throwing wide the black doors of night, and heralding that conquering glory at whose advent despair and darkness flee away.